Stories from China:
Fried Rice for the Soul

Stories from China:
Fried Rice for the Soul

Luke Wesley

Authentic

ATLANTA · LONDON · HYDERABAD

11   7 6 5 4 3

First published 2005 by Authentic Media,
9 Holdom Avenue, Bletchley, Milton Keynes, MK1 1QR, UK
and 129 Mobilization Drive, Waynesboro, GA 30830-4575, USA
www.authenticmedia.co.uk

British Library Cataloguing in Publication Data

A catalogue record for this book is available
from the British Library

ISBN   1-85078-638-0

Cover design by jaffa:design
Typeset by GCS, Leighton Buzzard, Beds.
Print Management by Adare Carwin

Contents

Dedication

To my Chinese friends,
through whom God has so richly blessed me.

Foreword

In the fall of 1994, during a Sunday worship service in Gang Wa Shi Church, Beijing, 1 was sitting in the sanctuary with about a thousand other members. We noticed the presence of many PSB (police) in civil dress. The director of the Beijing Religious Affairs Bureau (RAB) and the Chairman of the Beijing Three Self Patriotic Movement (TSPM) were sitting on the stage behind the pulpit. Pastor Yang Yudong was "too evangelical" and the church was growing "too fast," especially with so many youth who were supposed to be the successors of Socialism. The government had posted a notice on the church wall that Pastor Yang was retiring.

The congregation erupted when, suddenly, Pastor Yang Yudong appeared. The whole night he had hidden in a tunnel behind the stage. Listening to Pastor Yang's surprise farewell and stunned by his sudden presence, the director of the RAB went up and "persuaded" Pastor Yang to hand him the microphone. The 80-year-old chairman of the TSPM ironically told the congregation that Pastor Yang, in his 70s, was retired and no longer able to serve the church. Then the head of the state church preached a sermon entitled, "How the imperialists used the Chinese church to invade Chinese culture."

The same state church allows only one Christian magazine, one doctrine and appoints one set of leaders for *all Protestant Christians*. Two years later, in 1996, my wife Heidi and I were put into jail for two months because of "illegal evangelistic activities" (we planted a house church and established a Bible training center). Persecution is a reality that many Christians around the world face daily. The Apostle Paul wrote while imprisoned, "For it has been granted to you for the sake of Christ you should not only believe in him but also SUFFER for his sake" (Phil. 1:29 ESV).

Statistics show there may be as many as 60 to 100 million believers in China. They need Bibles! It took me one year to get a smuggled Bible from Hong Kong after I believed in Christ, in 1989. The only place to buy a Bible in China is in a large city where Bibles are only sold in a government-controlled TSPM church. In China's rural areas, where 80 percent of the population live; there are no Bibles available in bookstores.

This morning (October 26, 2006), I received a phone call from our China Aid investigator in China that a church in Xinjiang was raided by PSB while they were having a retreat. A Korean pastor, who is an American citizen, and 34 leaders are now being harshly interrogated. I have to stop writing here to start another campaign to "Remember them in chains" (Heb. 13:3).

It is a privilege, along with The Voice of the Martyrs, to present Luke Wesley's book containing the courage of China's Christians.

— Bob Fu
www.ChinaAid.org

Reverend Bob Fu is an ordained pastor and a PhD. candidate at Westminster Theological Seminary. He has testified before the U.S. Congress and the United Nations Human Rights Commission.

Introduction

It is now apparent that since the early 1980s the church in China has experienced unprecedented growth. Once viewed as an essentially foreign faith, Christianity has taken root in the Chinese soil – and it has blossomed. If the trends of the past two decades remain constant, by 2020 there will be more evangelical Christians in China than in any other country in the world.[1]

Observers in the West are still attempting to understand this burgeoning Christian movement and much is still unknown. It is evident that there is plenty to be learnt from the Chinese church, dynamic, multifaceted, and diverse as it is, and set within a nation of 1.3 billion people. We in the West would do well to take time to understand it more clearly. Such an undertaking might shed light on ourselves, our own strengths and weaknesses, and stimulate new insights into our understanding and application of God's word. In short, a greater understanding of the church in China might help us more fully comprehend and fulfil God's plans and purposes for our lives.

---

[1] Tony Lambert, *China's Christian Millions* (London: OMF/Monarch Books, 1999), 179. In this book Lambert offers what is by all accounts a conservative estimate of the number of evangelical Christians in China: 30–50 million. Most 'China watchers' in 2004 would agree that this figure is now nearer 60 million.

The devotional readings that follow are an attempt to help readers in the West learn from the experience of the Chinese church. They are based upon my experiences over roughly a ten-year period in China (1994–2004). The Chinese church has suffered much, but it is a powerful, vibrant and dynamic expression of the body of Christ in our world.

Chinese believers live in a world very different from our own. It is a world filled with obstacles and much opposition. And yet, believers in China are transforming this great nation with their bold witness and radically different lives. It is out of this unique context, and their response to it, that Chinese Christians are able to teach us so much. It is my hope that this book will stir your heart and enable you to learn from our brothers and sisters in China.

In order to set the stage for the meditations that follow, I begin with a brief overview of church life in China today.

The Church in China: A Brief Overview

On any given Sunday in any major city of China a foreign Christian can, if persistent, find a Protestant church and worship there openly with other Chinese believers. Bible schools and training centres can also be found functioning openly in most provinces and many cities. Bibles and a limited supply of other Christian books (including, for example, William Barclay's commentaries on the New Testament translated into Chinese) can be purchased in Christian bookshops affiliated with the Three Self Patriotic Movement (TSPM) churches. And yet, at the same time, we hear of intense persecution in China. We read stories of church leaders being beaten and imprisoned. We are told that Bibles are in short supply and thus desperately needed in China. How do we put it all together? How do we reconcile these apparently contradictory messages?

China is filled with many paradoxes and the question of religious persecution is one of them. In order to understand this important issue and the present realities that exist in China, we need to look at the broad and complex contours of church life in contemporary China. Some historical perspective will also be instructive.

The Ebb and Flow of History

Mao Zedong and the communist forces took control of mainland China in 1949. Since then the church has experienced many difficult periods. At times the persecution has been extremely intense, at other times less so. Initially, the official policy of the Chinese Communist Party (CCP) appears to have been one of allowing the church to gradually wither away. This policy was based on the assumption that in the new society ushered in by the CCP, religion in general, and the Christian church in particular, would become unnecessary and meaningless. In accordance with classical Marxist doctrine, it was felt that both would quickly fade away. When this did not happen, CCP policy shifted to a more aggressive stance, actively seeking to 'help' the church die away. More recently, at least since the early 1980s, the policy of the CCP has returned to the less aggressive but still basically hostile position of the early 1950s. In short, it is important to note that while the attitude of the CCP has been consistently hostile towards Christianity, it has fluctuated between periods of measured acceptance with imposed limitations on the one hand and zero tolerance enforced by active suppression on the other.

The most intense period of persecution was the decade of chaos and ferment – the Cultural Revolution (1966–76). This was a period of intense conflict and struggle in which Mao and his supporters mobilized the youth of the country in an attempt to attack their opponents, those who had become weary of the politicization of virtually every aspect of life in China, and to reassert their power. The young 'Red Guards' were whipped into a heated frenzy and encouraged to lash out at counter-revolutionary elements within Chinese society. Religion and particularly Christians and the church were major targets. During the Cultural Revolution every church in the country was closed, many pastors were imprisoned or, in some instances, killed, and the open practice of Christianity was brutally suppressed.

Fortunately today the situation in China is very different. While it is true that persecution continues to exist, it is also true that conditions for Christians have improved significantly. Today there are two forms of church life in China: churches which are recognized by the government – these generally belong to the TSPM – and the house churches, which do not submit to government regulations and control.

We often hear a black and white message: the registered or TSPM church is apostate and evil; the house church is pure and good. This is simplistic. Like so many facets of life in China, the truth is much more complex – God is at work in both sectors of the Chinese church. Moreover, the key to understanding the paradox of open churches and focused persecution in China lies in a clear appraisal of these two sectors of the Chinese church.

The TSPM Church and Government Interference

One cannot visit a TSPM church, get to know some of the church members, and leave feeling that God is not present. Although it is true that many TSPM church services are rather formal and lifeless, there is generally a strong sense of piety and faith. I remember one church service where an usher walked down the aisle brandishing a long stick. He used the stick to prod any sleepy believers out of their slumbering state. Although this church was not particularly alive, a number of strong young Christians worshipped there. There can be no doubt that many vital Christians worship in TSPM churches across China.

It is true, however, that churches recognized by the government face serious challenges. Although they are allowed to meet openly (thus you can find an open, functioning church in almost any major city in China), this recognition comes with a price. TSPM churches generally face the following restrictions:

1. *They must meet in designated places, at designated times, with designated leadership*. This means that while there are 'open' churches in China, they are very limited in number. For example, in one city of around three million people, there are only three open, Protestant churches. This is not unusual, but rather typical. Additionally, the development of ministry outside the confines of the church building – such as lay-led, small group Bible studies, for example – is severely restricted.

2. *The teaching of children or youth under 18 years of age in the church is generally prohibited*. Sunday school for children or special services for youth are exceedingly rare. It is evident that there is a conscious attempt on the part of the government to block these sorts of activities. It is touching to see young mothers struggle to keep their children from disrupting the service in TSPM churches. They simply have no alternative.

3. *It is illegal to evangelize outside the walls of the church.*
4. *It is illegal to use or possess Christian literature not published in China and approved by the Chinese government.*

The most significant of these restrictions, in my opinion, has to do with the selection of church leadership. The Chinese government has a say in who is selected to serve as pastors and leaders in the TSPM churches. A close friend of mine is a TSPM church leader. He has shared with me in a very open manner his own frustrations with working in the system. There have been times when he was so discouraged that he considered leaving the registered church and ministering in the house church setting. And yet, through all of the difficulties, he has remained inside and has had a significant impact in our region. On one occasion he told me that his greatest struggle with life in the TSPM was the fact that he had been asked to ordain people that he knew should not be ordained. It is evident that Christians in TSPM churches are not free to select their own leaders based on their spiritual character and giftedness. The government can and does intervene in the selection process. Thus pastors and leaders who are not spiritually qualified and who would not have been selected by the Christians they serve if they were given a choice, are occasionally selected and ordained. This problem appears to be more pronounced the higher one goes up the TSPM leadership ladder. Registered churches in the rural areas are often less impacted by government intervention.

It should be noted that the extent of government interference in the TSPM as well as the amount of energy exerted on suppressing house churches varies widely. The key factor here is the attitude of local government leaders. China is not a law-based society. For this reason the way in which guidelines on religious activity are interpreted and applied varies greatly. Everything depends on the perception and attitude of the person in charge. The law is essentially whatever the leader says it is. This is often difficult for westerners to understand. But it also explains why there is such variation in the level of religious freedom allowed from province to province and even county to county within China.

On one occasion a close friend who is also a leader in the TSPM unfolded a map of our province. He began to explain which counties were more open to religious activity and which were not. It was evident that the government leadership at the county level set the tone for religious conditions in their area. So, as my friend indicated, one county might offer considerable freedom for the TSPM church and even ignore significant house church activity, while another county may not tolerate any public Christian presence whatsoever.

Additionally, it should be noted that within the TSPM, pastors and church leaders vary widely in their willingness to buck the system. After a Sunday morning service in a large TSPM church in one populous city, I shared a meal with one of the pastors. He was an older man and obviously a senior leader in the church. While we ate I asked him, 'What are the pressing issues confronting the Chinese church?' His response was extremely revealing. He indicated that there was a significant gulf developing between the older, more cautious pastors who had experienced first-hand the reality of persecution, and the younger, more aggressive pastors who had not yet witnessed the possible consequences of crossing government-established boundaries. This man identified with the older, more cautious pastors. He had seen too much.

I have found that rural TSPM Christians and church leaders are often quite autonomous and very willing to 'break the rules' in order to see the ministry of the church expand. This is less true of TSPM leaders in the larger cities who operate under greater scrutiny. Nevertheless, there are some notable exceptions in this regard as well.

Of course, the attitudes of the TSPM church leaders in a given area and the past experience of their house church counterparts together impact on the nature of TSPM and house church relations. In some instances there are very positive relationships between the two groups with house church believers occasionally attending TSPM services. I have also seen TSPM pastors support house church groups in their region in a variety of ways. Yet this sort of positive relationship is not the norm. The large house church networks, which have a long history of persecution and suppression, do not hold the TSPM in high regard. Often with good reason, they view the TSPM as a tool of the government and link it together with their persecutors. And yet, their antagonistic approach to the TSPM can often be a self-fulfilling prophecy. When they attack the local TSPM church and encourage believers to leave and join their groups, TSPM pastors understandably become very upset. These issues are complex and rooted in personal histories and entrenched attitudes.

In spite of the restrictions outlined above, the TSPM church is alive and growing in many areas. The TSPM churches tend to be conservative and evangelical in their theology and, as I have noted, they often defy government restrictions and bear witness boldly. Some of the readings that follow testify to this fact. Of course there is another side to church life within the TSPM, one that is not so bright. This is also illustrated in some of the stories that follow.

The House Church and Persecution

Largely because of government intervention and the restrictions noted above, most Christians in China have chosen not to worship in registered churches, but in house churches. There is a cost: they face intimidation, harassment and the fear of arrest. Nevertheless, the house church is booming. In 1949 there were less than one million Protestant believers. Now, conservative estimates would suggest that there are at least 60 million. Most of this growth has occurred in the last 15 years, especially since the Tiananmen Square incident in 1989. Almost every believer I know has come to Christ since then. One friend stated, 'When that happened, I knew the government had lied to me.' He began to search for answers.

The simplicity and power of worship in the house church setting is deeply moving. There is something wonderful and powerful about small groups of believers gathering together, in spite of the threat of persecution, to worship Christ. Everyone contributes, everyone shares.

People usually come to faith in these settings, not in response to a specific appeal, but rather after the meeting concludes. After the meeting there is almost always an informal time of fellowship and regularly someone will approach one of the leaders and, in various forms, say, 'I experienced something different, something wonderful here. I want to become a Christian. Tell me how I can become a follower of Jesus.' Several of the meditations that follow seek to capture some of the power of these house church meetings.

The house church movement is maturing. There are now a number of large house church networks that are national in scope and highly organized. At least five of these networks number three million or more believers each. These networks are transforming China. They are also targeted by the government and severely persecuted.

In the city in which I live there are many house church groups. The majority of these groups are small and have little structure or connection to other Christian groups. They are, for the most part, ignored by local officials. However, the large house church groups, which have extensive networks connecting churches across many provinces, are viewed as a serious threat by the government. They are large and organized, therefore they must be suppressed. This is the real locus of persecution in China.

On one occasion I had the privilege of meeting with eight leaders of a large house church network. This network numbers well over three million believers and is growing rapidly. For this reason, it has experienced intense persecution. We had a wonderful time of sharing and prayer. Several things amazed me about this group. First, they were so young! All but the senior leader were still in their twenties and most had been in ministry for at least ten years. Second, they were all, with one exception, women. The Chinese church is about 80 per cent female. Women are a crucial and indeed dominant force in the Chinese church. If you take away the women, you don't have much of a church. Third, they had all, with one exception, spent time in prison.

Yet in spite of this kind of hardship, there is a boldness and joy which characterizes the house church believers. This aspect of their faith is illustrated in a number of the testimonies and songs that follow.

Conclusion

Church life in China today is filled with paradoxes. While Christians meet openly for Sunday morning worship in TSPM churches, house church believers are arrested and imprisoned. One city or region may experience considerable freedom, while another city or region allows little or no public expression of the faith. Some house church Christians are ignored, while others, especially those associated with large networks, are closely monitored and targeted for suppression. Clearly the context in China is complex and it defies simplistic, black and white judgements or descriptions. Nevertheless, my brief summary of the church and persecution in China has illuminated the following points:

1. Since the communist takeover in 1949, the church in China has faced many difficult periods of persecution, some more intense than others. Fortunately, the dark days of the Cultural Revolution are past and today the situation is much improved.
2. While TSPM churches meet openly, they do so with significant limitations imposed upon them.
3. Christians who worship in TSPM churches and their leaders are often godly people who openly identify themselves as Christians and seek to impact their country for Christ.
4. Nevertheless, the vast majority of Christians in China choose to worship in house churches that do not submit to government regulations and control.
5. These house churches, especially the networks that are large and highly organized, are targeted by the government and are the object of deliberate and sustained persecution.

We have noted that the dark days of the Cultural Revolution are a thing of the past. Nevertheless, persecution is an all too real experience for many Christians in China today. It continues to exist and often in very flagrant and extreme forms. And yet, in the midst of this persecution, God has ministered to and through the Chinese church in powerful ways. It would appear that persecution and power often go hand in hand.

My prayer for Christians in the West is that we too would experience some of this power. I trust that the following meditations will encourage all of us to hunger after this dynamic work of the Holy Spirit in our lives; and that he will work in and through us the same way as he has in the lives of countless Chinese believers.

Meditation #1:
The 'Iron Rice Bowl' Reunion

Paul and his companions travelled throughout the region of Phrygia and Galatia, having been kept by the Holy Spirit from preaching the word in the province of Asia. When they came to the border of Mysia, they tried to enter Bithynia, but the Spirit of Jesus would not allow them to. So they passed by Mysia and went down to Troas. During the night Paul had a vision of a man of Macedonia standing and begging him, 'Come over to Macedonia and help us.' After Paul had seen the vision, we got ready at once to leave for Macedonia, concluding that God had called us to preach the gospel to them (Acts 16:6–10).

As my wife and I sought to settle into life in China, one priority was to obtain two sturdy bicycles. To be in China without a bicycle is a bit like being stranded on a desert island, isolated and cut off from the world around you. I inherited my old bike from a friend, but we had to purchase a new two-wheeler for my wife. So, bright and early one morning I set out to buy my wife's bike. After finding, bargaining a bit, and then buying a very reliable model, I proceeded to pedal to the appropriate government office with high hopes of obtaining the obligatory licence. This can be (and on this day was) a real ordeal. I pedalled hard for 30 minutes, knowing that time was short. If I didn't make it to the office by 11:30 am, I would have to wait until the post lunch-break opening at 2:30 pm.

Many aspects of life in China move slowly. This situation is intensified by what is often called the 'iron rice bowl' mentality – a reference to lacklustre performance resulting from the knowledge that one's job is secure (no matter what!). With all the changes taking place in China, the days of the 'iron rice bowl' appear to be numbered – but sadly, these changes had not yet impacted this particular government office. I was elated to find that my huffing, puffing and hard pedalling had paid off: I arrived at 11:15 am. I squeezed my way through a human wall and into the office yard, noting a sign which clearly stated that the office was open until 11:30 am. Yet, to my dismay, I quickly saw that all the government officials had already left for a protracted lunch-break. I was told I would have to come back three hours later having already spent almost an hour on my bike. The 'iron rice bowl' had triumphed!

I stood dejectedly outside the office gate, wondering what to do. At that moment I heard a friendly voice call my name and Wang Dong[1], a friend from a previous visit to the area, appeared. He had a big grin on his face and, before I knew what was happening, he said rather loudly, 'I'm a Christian! Last year I became a Christian! Thank you for the New Testament you gave me.'

I knew Wang Dong as a very sharp university graduate. We had frequently played basketball together, and I had come to realize that he was interested in the message of the Bible. When I left China on one occasion I gave him a going away present, a New Testament. Other Christians continued to share with Wang Dong and then, one day, he committed his life to the Lord. What a joy it was now to hear of his conversion!

---

[1] The names of many of the Chinese people cited in this book have been altered in order to protect their identity.

Wang Dong quickly introduced me to his friend, Xiao Yang, who was also a new Christian. The three of us spent the next several hours discussing their conversions, their involvement in Christian outreach (Wang Dong had recently led two of his friends to the Lord), and various themes from the Bible. Their enthusiasm and hunger for the word of God was refreshing. How glad I was that the 'iron rice bowl' had indeed won out, enabling this unexpected reunion to take place.

Lord, I acknowledge that you delight to lead and guide me in ways that will bring you glory and bless others. I offer my life, my time, and my schedule to you this day. Bring those unexpected surprises, those unanticipated interruptions into my life and allow me to see them for what they are: opportunities that you have brought my way. Use me this day for your glory.

Meditation #2:
The Red Triangle

In Damascus there was a disciple named Ananias. The Lord called to him in a vision, 'Ananias!'

'Yes, Lord,' he answered.

The Lord told him, 'Go to the house of Judas on Straight Street and ask for a man from Tarsus named Saul, for he is praying. In a vision he has seen a man named Ananias come and place his hands on him to restore his sight.'

'Lord,' Ananias answered, 'I have heard many reports about this man and all the harm he has done to your saints in Jerusalem. And he has come here with authority from the chief priests to arrest all who call on your name.'

But the Lord said to Ananias, 'Go! This man is my chosen instrument to carry my name before the Gentiles and their kings and before the people of Israel. I will show him how much he must suffer for my name.'

Then Ananias went to the house and entered it. Placing his hands on Saul, he said, 'Brother Saul, the Lord – Jesus, who appeared to you on the road as you were coming here – has sent me so that you may see again and be filled with the Holy Spirit.' Immediately, something like scales fell from Saul's eyes, and he could see again. He got up and was baptised, and after taking some food, he regained his strength.

Saul spent several days with the disciples in Damascus. At once he began to preach in the synagogues that Jesus is the Son of God (Acts 9:10–20).

I had just returned home from a busy schedule of meetings in Hong Kong. I had expected to meet my good friend, Mr Huang. Instead, Huang's wife, Wang Mei, appeared. She sat down on our sofa and burst into tears. After composing herself she explained that Huang was near death. Shortly after we left for Hong Kong, Huang began to feel sick. When his condition grew worse he was admitted into a local hospital. Unfortunately, the doctors were unable to diagnose the problem. Three weeks later, now in his third hospital, Huang's problem was confirmed: a severe case of hepatitis. His body had swollen to grotesque proportions. The young, capable doctor pulled Wang Mei aside and said, 'It is too late, we cannot save him.'

Although Huang was a Christian, Wang Mei was not. She had many intellectual objections to the Christian faith. But now, in the midst of this crisis, her Marxist world-view was of little comfort. She responded eagerly when we suggested that we pray together. As we prayed we sensed God was at work. I scribbled a quick note to Huang reminding him that God had called him to bring the gospel to his people. God was not through with him yet! I tucked the note into a New Testament and handed it to Wang Mei, hopeful that she might have opportunities to read it in the hospital.

I must admit, however, I had mixed feelings. On the one hand, I wondered how God could let this happen? Huang was my closest Chinese friend, a young man whom I felt had tremendous potential to impact China in a significant way for the kingdom of God. Now the doctors offered little or no hope for his survival. He was extremely bloated, yellow and near death. The doctors wouldn't even allow us to visit him. On the other hand, it seemed that this was the perfect opportunity for God to intervene and reveal his presence and power to Huang's family, particularly his wife. Yet the situation was so desperate, it was difficult to remain confident and hopeful.

About two weeks later, I went to visit Huang for the first time. When I saw him it was evident that God was at work. The doctors were amazed: he had not only survived, but was recovering very quickly. They told Huang, 'A power is at work here which we do not understand.' Amazed at his peaceful attitude in the face of death, they attributed his remarkable recovery to 'the strength of his spirit'. Yet Huang knew the true source of this power. He declared to us (and later to his non-Christian friends): 'God has healed me!'

Over the course of his stay in the hospital, four men with similar symptoms in turn occupied a bed in the adjacent room. All four came and all four died. Huang and Wang Mei were powerfully aware of the miracle God had performed.

Huang explained how this event had affected their lives. Daily, Wang Mei read out loud the Bible we had given her in order to comfort him. This had a significant impact on Wang Mei, as well as Huang. Huang began to weep as he described how he had been praying for Wang Mei for four years, and now, at last, she had given her heart to the Lord. One day, after a long conversation in which Huang beautifully dealt with her intellectual questions, Wang Mei went home to sleep. In a dream she had a vision of Jesus, dressed in white, taking Huang by the hand and raising him up. She sensed real peace. The next day, she asked Huang to teach her how to pray and committed her life to the Lord.

Huang too was changed. He began to speak with new urgency about the need to spread the good news. He also began to prayerfully ask how God might use him. There was a fresh sense of God's call upon his life to bring the gospel to his people.

Later I had the joy of escorting Huang home after he had received a clean bill of health. On the way out of the hospital he nodded to a chart hanging on the wall. Small pegs represented the beds of patients, and on some, little red triangles indicated that the situation was 'critical'. Huang said, 'One of these red triangles used to mark my bed, but not any longer!' We rejoice at the richness of God's grace and the vastness of his power, both so beautifully revealed in the experience of this Chinese family. For Huang, the red triangle is gone, but the powerful presence of God remains. Now, a number of years later, Huang is a gifted and powerful house church evangelist.

Lord, I rejoice in the way in which you reveal your love and power to me. Sometimes I see you in dramatic moments of healing and wonderful displays of power. Sometimes you reveal yourself to me in quiet and subtle ways, unnoticed by those around. And yet you are surely there, seeking me, chasing after me, and finding me in the midst of my need. Give me eyes to see you and your purposes for my life. Change me into the person you want me to be.

Meditation #3:
Representing the Love of Christ

For Christ's love compels us, because we are convinced that one died for all, and therefore all died. And he died for all, that those who live should no longer live for themselves but for him who died for them and was raised again.

So from now on we regard no one from a worldly point of view. Though we once regarded Christ in this way, we do so no longer. Therefore, if anyone is in Christ, he is a new creation; the old has gone, the new has come! All this is from God, who reconciled us to himself through Christ and gave us the ministry of reconciliation: that God was reconciling the world to himself in Christ, not counting men's sins against them. And he has committed to us the message of reconciliation. We are therefore Christ's ambassadors, as though God were making his appeal through us. We implore you on Christ's behalf: Be reconciled to God (2 Cor. 5:14–20).

Several years ago, I along with several family members, including my in-laws (missionaries to Latin America for over 40 years), had the privilege of meeting together with house church leaders associated with a large house church network. The top leader, along with seven other key leaders, was present.

We had wonderful times of prayer and fellowship with this group. We were able to encourage them as well as be encouraged. During one time of prayer, my mother-in-law felt impressed to wrap her arms around several of the ladies and pray for them. She shared this with me as I had the task of translating for her. I hesitated, concerned that this might be culturally inappropriate. This was Beijing, not Mexico City! Latins are very expressive and comfortable with physical displays of affection, but the Chinese are not. As I pondered the situation, my mother-in-law, who is absolutely irrepressible, jumped up and began to hug each one of the ladies and pray for them. One by one, as she hugged them, the ladies burst into tears. It was a very moving and meaningful time. The Holy Spirit began to bring a special sense of comfort and peace.

Afterwards, one of the ladies shared why my mother-in-law's hug had been so meaningful. She described how she had faced rejection all her life. When she became a Christian, her family disowned her. As a young teenager she began to travel and preach in villages. As a result, she faced tremendous hardships and persecution. She had experienced so many difficulties, so much rejection, that she had recently asked the Lord to reveal his love to her in a special way. With tears streaming down her face she said, 'When your mother-in-law wrapped her arms around me, I felt Jesus was embracing me.'

Lord, I ask that today you would help me represent your love to those around me. I know that I will meet people who need encouragement, people who need to be directed towards or reminded of your love for them. Help me represent you to them. Allow me to be your ambassador. Help me not to be afraid to take risks. Help me not to be bound by my own weaknesses or the limits of my own strength and knowledge. Lead me and use me, I pray. Enable me to reflect your love and grace this day.

Meditation #4:
A House Church is Born

For this reason, ever since I heard about your faith in the Lord Jesus and your love for all the saints, I have not stopped giving thanks for you, remembering you in my prayers. I keep asking that the God of our Lord Jesus Christ, the glorious Father, may give you the Spirit of wisdom and revelation, so that you may know him better. I pray also that the eyes of your heart may be enlightened in order that you may know the hope to which he has called you, the riches of his glorious inheritance in the saints, and his incomparably great power for us who believe. That power is like the working of his mighty strength, which he exerted in Christ when he raised him from the dead and seated him at his right hand in the heavenly realms, far above all rule and authority, power and dominion, and every title that can be given, not only in the present age but also in the one to come. And God placed all things under his feet and appointed him to be head over everything for the church, which is his body, the fullness of him who fills everything in every way (Eph. 1:15–23).

On one occasion several house church leaders and I travelled down to a region south of our city where we met with two fledgling groups. A leader from the city group had led a young woman from this rural area to the Lord the previous year. Full of the Spirit and excited about her new-found faith, she began to share the gospel with her friends. Now, about a year later, a group of believers was meeting regularly in her home for worship and instruction in the Bible. Another smaller group had also formed in a nearby city. The believers, all new in the faith, asked our little band to help give them direction and instruction. So, although at the time we didn't know what we would find, on the appointed day leaders from our little house church piled into a vehicle and travelled down to the village to meet with these new brothers and sisters in the Lord.

We parked the vehicle on the outskirts of the village, and then our group of five adults hiked up the hill to the meeting point where the believers had gathered. As we ascended the rough steps of the muddy path, we began to hear music – the beautiful sound of many voices praising God. Our steps quickened as our excitement grew. When we entered the little courtyard, we were amazed to find a group of 40 already present, eager to hear from the word of God and to share their testimonies. We had a wonderful day, filled with teaching, preaching, fellowship and encouragement. As a result, seven people came to the Lord. Thankfully, this trend continued. Almost every week we saw people make decisions to follow Christ. Often, after a service, they would come and say that they had been touched by a prayer, a testimony, or the message and that they too wanted to follow Christ.

The key to the growth of the church in China is clearly the bold, Spirit-inspired witness of the Chinese believers. On one occasion, a visiting friend who is also a medical doctor, spoke to the city group in a special meeting. Since many members of the church group serve in hospitals, as a doctor my friend was able to relate in a special way. During this meeting, one of the ladies asked how bold she should be in sharing her faith with a particular patient. The patient was a young girl who was scheduled

for heart surgery. We encouraged our friend to follow the
prompting of the Holy Spirit and pray with her. The
following Sunday I learnt that our friend had indeed
shared the gospel with this young girl and she had
accepted the Lord! Her surgery had also gone very well.
Several church members and I had the joy of meeting
with this new believer for a time of prayer later that day. I
was moved by the boldness of my Chinese friends as I
saw them encourage the non-Christian doctors to give
God the glory for the successful surgery.

The house church has continued to prosper. Later we
held a joint meeting of several groups. It was a wonderful
open-air meeting in a remote valley. A Chinese friend and
I both spoke from the word. At one point during the
service we all shared the Lord's supper. When the bread
was passed out, I noticed three men who did not participate. One had earlier identified himself as a member of
the local Public Security Bureau (the Chinese police). This
made me a bit nervous, so after the service I enquired
about him. My Chinese friends told me not to worry, he
was a close friend of several of the believers. This man
had been deeply moved by the fellowship and worship.
But when the other two men who had not participated in
the communion service approached me, I again began to
feel uneasy, that is until they asked me how they too
could follow Jesus. God is indeed building his church!

Lord, I praise you and give you glory, for you indeed are
building your church. In the midst of opposition,
persecution and every hardship, you are impacting lives
and bringing believers together so that we may worship
you. I thank you because you have called me to be a part
of your church. You have called me to worship you, to
encourage my brothers and sisters, and to reach out to
others in your name. I rejoice because I am a part of your

church – a church that includes people from every nation, including China. I pray that you might help me encourage the brothers and sisters in my home church and reach out to those around me who do not know you. I also pray for the church in China. I praise you for the marvellous way you are building your church in this great land. Bless the church in China, Lord, strengthen it and enable it to prosper.

Meditation #5:
The Gate Lady

Now an angel of the Lord said to Philip, 'Go south to the road – the desert road – that goes down from Jerusalem to Gaza.' So he started out, and on his way he met an Ethiopian eunuch, an important official in charge of all the treasury of Candace, queen of the Ethiopians. This man had gone to Jerusalem to worship, and on his way home was sitting in his chariot reading the book of Isaiah the prophet. The Spirit told Philip, 'Go to that chariot and stay near it.'

Then Philip ran up to the chariot and heard the man reading Isaiah the prophet. 'Do you understand what you are reading?' Philip asked.

'How can I,' he said, 'unless someone explains it to me?' So he invited Philip to come up and sit with him (Acts 8:26–31).

It had been a busy day trying to help friends, fresh from the USA, find an apartment to rent. Our apartment complex was rumoured to have openings, but it was usually difficult to make contact with the owners. I knew that the little old lady who watched over the gate of our large complex would be the key. We call her 'the gate lady'. A small lady, barely four and a half feet tall, thin and wiry, she embodies the term 'busy body', for she seems to know everything that takes place within her realm. Our relationship had always been cordial – you definitely want to be on good terms with 'the gate lady'!

– but pretty much restricted to matters of business. As I entered her little office-home next to the gate, I noticed that her hand was wrapped in a bandage. While we discussed the apartment situation, I felt the Holy Spirit tugging at my heart, urging me to pray for her. A million and one objections raced through my mind. I really didn't know this lady that well. What if she became offended and reported my prayer to the police? What if she tried to have us kicked out of the country? These fears were not unreasonable given the nature of life in the People's Republic of China, but I felt the Holy Spirit prompt me to move beyond these concerns. So I asked her, 'Can I pray with you?' I continued, 'I am a Christian and in our home we often bring our needs to Jesus, God's son.' She beamed a big smile at me. It was the first time I had seen her smile. She said that she would like that very much. I began my prayer by thanking God for his love for us. I uttered the words, 'Lord, you love us.'

The gate lady chimed in and added a declaration of her own, 'Yes, you love us!'

After the prayer I immediately sensed that our relationship had changed. Previously we had related to each other on a rather impersonal level, discussing matters that were a necessary part of our daily activities, but little else. Now, however, we were friends. Concern, compassion, and, above all, simple obedience (i.e. the willingness to follow the prompting of the Spirit in spite of the risk) had made the difference. Our gate lady is not yet a believer, but I am confident it is only a matter of time. She and the Lord taught me a great lesson that day.

Lord, I marvel at the fact that you are not only willing, but that you truly desire to use me to glorify your name and bless others. I thank you for including me in your mission to redeem your creation. Allow me to see those around

me as you see them. Enable me to reach out to others with
concern and compassion. Help me to be sensitive to the
leading of your Spirit in my life. Above all, help me to be
willing to lay aside my fears, my cautions, my personal
comfort, and in obedience follow you.

Meditation #6:
The Journey

As for you, you were dead in your transgressions and sins, in which you used to live when you followed the ways of this world and of the ruler of the kingdom of the air, the spirit who is now at work in those who are disobedient. All of us also lived among them at one time, gratifying the cravings of our sinful nature and following its desires and thoughts. Like the rest, we were by nature objects of wrath. But because of his great love for us, God, who is rich in mercy, made us alive with Christ even when we were dead in transgressions – it is by grace you have been saved. And God raised us up with Christ and seated us with him in the heavenly realms in Christ Jesus, in order that in the coming ages he might show the incomparable riches of his grace, expressed in his kindness to us in Christ Jesus. For it is by grace you have been saved, through faith – and this not from yourselves, it is the gift of God – not by works, so that no one can boast. For we are God's workmanship, created in Christ Jesus to do good works, which God prepared in advance for us to do (Eph. 2:1–10).

We hiked up the dirt path that led to the house where the Christians had gathered. The simple home made of mud brick and plaster includes a kitchen, a living room, a bedroom, and another room measuring approximately 25 feet long and 10 feet wide – the church. The rooms link together in an L-shaped pattern and a courtyard edged by a six foot wall completes the rectangle. Normally the sound of singing and worship greets us as we enter the courtyard. On this day, however, we had arrived early before the hymns had started. We were to meet with a group of church leaders for a time of teaching and prayer. We found our seats on wicker stools and wooden benches, while a dog slept under the rough wooden table in the centre of the room. The meeting began with prayer, followed by a time of worship and instruction.

Thirty minutes into the meeting, a man of no more than 35 years of age entered the room. He slumped down onto a wooden bench near the door. His face and bearing mirrored his sadness and despair. Mr Wang was indeed distraught. Just four days earlier his 17-year-old daughter had passed away. This compounded the grief he felt over the loss of his wife, who had died some years ago. With his wife and daughter gone, Mr Wang was without hope. He had tried to drown his sorrows with drink and the previous day, in a drunken stupor, had somehow managed to stumble into the church. The believers invited him to come back when sober in order to attend our meeting.

The topic of the day was repentance, its meaning and significance. As various ones shared, the hope of the gospel was made clear. Towards the end of the service, Mr Wang indicated that he was ready to repent of his sins and accept Christ as Lord and Saviour. It was a wonderful scene. The band of believers gathered around Mr Wang in prayer, many of us laying our hands upon him. Together we cried out to God for his comfort and strength. Mr Wang prayed the sinner's prayer and his countenance changed. He had crossed over from death to life. His face reflected the wonder and the glory of this incredible journey.

Lord, I praise you for your incredible love and for the life you have given me. I acknowledge that once I was dead, enslaved by sin, and living without hope. Now, however, because of your grace, I truly live. I live in freedom, able to worship and please you. I live with hope, because I am now able to fulfil the very purpose for which I was created: to worship you and to bring glory to your name. You have created me to do good works in the name of Christ. I ask that this day you would empower me to do this very thing. Enable me to reflect the strength, the joy and the peace of the new life you have given me. Thank you for making it possible for me to journey with you and to cross over from death to life.

Meditation #7:
A Christian Wedding

Be imitators of God, therefore, as dearly loved children and live a life of love, just as Christ loved us and gave himself up for us as a fragrant offering and sacrifice to God. ...

Wives, submit to your husbands as to the Lord. For the husband is the head of the wife as Christ is the head of the church, his body, of which he is the Saviour. Now as the church submits to Christ, so also wives should submit to their husbands in everything.

Husbands, love your wives, just as Christ loved the church and gave himself up for her to make her holy, cleansing her by the washing with water through the word, and to present her to himself as a radiant church, without stain or wrinkle or any other blemish, but holy and blameless. In this same way, husbands ought to love their wives as their own bodies. He who loves his wife loves himself (Eph. 5:1–2, 22–28).

A Chinese friend asked me to officiate at her wedding. She also asked if my wife and I would be willing to provide some pre-marital counselling to the young couple. We gladly accepted, asking the Lord to help us be a source of encouragement and blessing.

As it turned out, we had a wonderful time with the couple during our counselling sessions. Their obvious love for each other and the Lord was a blessing to us and, as we shared, many happy memories of our own early days together flooded back. In our city there are very few couples in which both husband and wife are Christians so it was especially encouraging to hear this fine couple declare their commitment to each other and to Christ.

The wedding itself was a rich blend of Chinese and western wedding traditions, but above all, it was a time of bold witness for Christ. Many non-Christians were present and the message of the reconciling love of Christ was clearly proclaimed. I gave a charge to the couple in Chinese and, with God's grace, was able to share what God had laid on my heart in an intelligible way. I also had the joy of praying a prayer of blessing and dedication for them. Many of their friends shared strong testimonies and they themselves spoke of Christ's love in a clear and compelling way. The ceremony was both moving and meaningful. After witnessing the emptiness of secular weddings in China – usually conducted in restaurants and marked by a lot of booze and loud music – and the beauty and depth of this one, I could understand why a number of Chinese have been drawn to Christ through attending Christian weddings.

Lord, I praise and worship you because you are the Faithful One. You are committed to me and have demonstrated this so wonderfully on the cross. Because you are committed to me, I can be committed to others, including my wife, my family, and my friends. You are my model and you are the source of my strength. Help me seek the good of others, even if it involves sacrifice on my part. Enable me to be a good spouse, a good parent and a good friend. Give me strength so that my relationships with others might reflect your sacrificial love and bring glory to you. I affirm again this day my commitment to you and to your purposes for my life.

Meditation #8:
Water and Wind

On the first day of the week, very early in the morning, the women took the spices they had prepared and went to the tomb. They found the stone rolled away from the tomb, but when they entered, they did not find the body of the Lord Jesus. While they were wondering about this, suddenly two men in clothes that gleamed like lightning stood beside them. In their fright the women bowed down with their faces to the ground, but the men said to them, 'Why do you look for the living among the dead? He is not here; he has risen! Remember how he told you, while he was still with you in Galilee: "The Son of Man must be delivered into the hands of sinful men, be crucified and on the third day be raised again."' Then they remembered his words (Lk. 24:1–8).

Rays of sunlight sliced through the tall trees, bringing warmth and light to the hill that our group of 50 occupied. A gentle breeze blew across the face of the lake that stretched out before us. The lake's quiet waters reminded us that the city was far away. But we were not here to enjoy the scenery. It was Easter morning. We had come to celebrate the resurrection of our Lord.

We found our place on the side of the hill as the musicians began to lead us in songs of praise. The time of worship was very special, as normally we were not all able to meet together. In a small apartment in the city space is limited and often the volume of praise must be contained. But now, together and out in the open, the joy was visible, almost tangible, and the praises rang. And then, as the worship reached its crescendo, as if one voice we all shouted in Chinese, 'Jesus is risen! He is risen indeed!'

At that moment I began to thank the Lord for the way in which he had led and blessed us these past years. I was reminded that this service, this incredible scene, was an answer to prayer. To worship together with this wonderful group, to declare the reality of the resurrection surrounded by Chinese brothers and sisters – this was truly the fulfilment of a dream.

As the time of worship came to a close, two Chinese adults expressed their desire to commit their lives to Christ. A Christian brother, himself a government official, had brought them to the meeting. The two visitors were moved by the purity of the fellowship and the sincerity of the worship. They had also been challenged by the proclamation of the risen Christ. I had the joy of leading our two new friends in a prayer of repentance and consecration. When I opened my eyes, I saw their faces reflecting the new reality: they had entered into the kingdom of God.

After the service, we all gathered together to share a meal of fellowship. The believers brought a rich assortment of food – nothing is so varied and interesting as a Chinese meal. When the eating and conversations subsided, the group moved down to the lake and the baptismal service began. Songs and prayers punctuated the powerful testimonies of the 14 people who were baptized that day. After each testimony, the waters rippled as young believers publicly declared their allegiance to Christ. Warm sunshine and a soft breeze greeted the Christians emerging from the water. It was Easter, a day to remember.

Lord, I declare the truth that has been passed down through the ages, the message that is filled with hope and life: You are risen! You are risen indeed! You are not dead, not merely a figure of the past. You live and you are actively at work in the world and in my life. I worship and praise you, for through your death and resurrection you have defeated the power of death, sin and Satan. I rejoice in the marvellous victory that you have won. I give thanks for the wondrous power that you have unleashed in the world and in my life. I pray that I would live with a fresh awareness of the life-giving power that you have placed in my life through the Holy Spirit. Today, let my life reflect this incredible reality: your resurrection power is at work in me!

Meditation #9:
A Part of the Family

You are all sons of God through faith in Christ Jesus, for all
of you who were baptised into Christ have clothed yourselves with Christ. There is neither Jew nor Greek, slave nor
free, male nor female, for you are all one in Christ Jesus. If
you belong to Christ, then you are Abraham's seed, and
heirs according to the promise (Gal. 3:26–29).

It was a beautiful Sunday morning when we set out for
the forest area near our city. A visiting evangelist from the
Miao minority group, Brother Long, travelled with me
and an American friend to the meeting point. On arrival
we joined up with around 80 of our house church friends
who had gathered together for a special celebration and
service. We scouted out a quiet, secluded spot and the
service began. After a refreshing time of worship, my
American friend delivered a powerful message on
'overcoming difficulties' from Philippians 1:12–26. Then
the Miao minister, Brother Long, shared about his recent
trip to seven poor Miao churches in a neighbouring
province. He began by noting that his people are
generally looked down upon by other groups in China,
especially the dominant Han majority. He said that
normally there would be no opportunity for him to speak
to a group of largely Han, educated city-dwellers like the
present group. However, Brother Long declared, 'Our
faith in Christ has changed all of that. In Christ, we are all

one family.' In this setting, marked by the Spirit's presence, the Miao brother felt at ease, a member of the family!

Brother Long went on to describe his recent experiences in these seven, remote villages. He highlighted the desperate need of one village for a church building. He also detailed how Christians in another village had started a much-needed school, but were struggling to support the project. They had four teachers, each of whom received about four US dollars per month. After Brother Long had finished speaking, one young Han Chinese believer challenged the group to prayerfully consider what the Holy Spirit might be saying to us concerning these needs and how we might help. We ended with a stirring time of prayer. Many came after the service with special needs and asked for prayer as well. These included one young man about 30 years of age who was a drug addict, but who had recently committed his life to Christ.

When the service had ended, we discovered that the church had given over 5,100 RMB (around US $610) towards the needs of the minority Christians. In view of the fact that most of these Chinese believers earn about US $100 per month, I felt this was a tremendous response. This house church really has a heart for missions!

Lord, I am so thankful that your family is large, very large. It is so large that it embraces or will embrace people from every tribe and every nation, people from every language group. And I rejoice because as we enter into your family, you make us one. You make us members of one family united in our common experience of your grace and love. I pray that today you would help me demonstrate your love for people who may be different from me – whether the differences be racial, ethnic, linguistic, or even socio-economic in character. Help me anticipate in my relationships here and now what life in your kingdom will be like one day when together people from every tribe and nation live in harmony under your rule. Help me be like the Chinese house church Christians who were able to see beyond the normal prejudices of their society and receive a Miao evangelist as a brother, a member of the family.

Meditation #10:
Set Our Hearts On Fire

'Be strong and courageous, because you will lead these people to inherit the land I swore to their forefathers to give them. Be strong and very courageous. Be careful to obey all the law my servant Moses gave you; do not turn from it to the right or to the left, that you may be successful wherever you go. Do not let this Book of the Law depart from your mouth; meditate on it day and night, so that you may be careful to do everything written in it. Then you will be prosperous and successful. Have I not commanded you? Be strong and courageous. Do not be terrified; do not be discouraged, for the LORD your God will be with you wherever you go' (Josh. 1:6–9).

The following two songs and the others that grace the pages of this book are my English translations of songs found in Lu Xiaomin's collection of songs entitled, *Sounds of the Heart*. Lu Xiaomin and her songs are known and loved by house church groups throughout China. I asked one Chinese friend how many believers knew about these songs. He exclaimed, 'All the house churches sing them!' *Sounds of the Heart* is a recently updated and expanded version of *Songs of Canaan*, Lu Xiaomin's previous and hugely popular song book. *Sounds of the Heart* contains 900 songs and is the closest thing to an 'official' song book that exists in the house churches in China today. In view of their popularity and impact, the songs penned by Lu Xiaomin are an important insight into Chinese Christianity. I have found them to be quite different from most Christian songs in the West, but powerful and full of inspiration.

Lord We Ask You, Set Our Hearts on Fire for China

Lord we ask you, set our hearts on fire for China
  Set our hearts on fire for China
Look at the Chinese church
  Take a look at your servants
They have truly endured many attacks
  They have weathered baptisms of wind and rain
But from the beginning they have never been afraid
  They have with steadfastness never wavered
Nor worried on the barren threshing floor
  And still from inside and out the pressure comes
Going south, rushing north, they stumble through
    hardships
  Not remaining long in any place
Lord, if this is your will
  I will joyfully thank and praise you
Even with fear over head like black clouds
  And thorny bushes under our feet
We will preach the gospel around the world.[1]

The Love of Jesus is the Reason

The love of Jesus is the reason we live bravely
  The needs of lost souls are the reason we live with
    determination

---

[1] Lu Xiaomin, *Sounds of the Heart* [*Xin Ling Zhi Sheng*] (underground house church publication, 2003), 652 (Song #592).

We do not fear setbacks and attacks
　　Wind and rain refine our character
Rain dampens our clothes
　　Snow covers our body
But we do not speak of fatigue or hardship
　　We are Christians
Our whole life we will serve the Lord
　　　The whole world watches the messengers and takes
note.[2]

Lord, give me the boldness and courage reflected in these songs. Grant to me the dedication and courage which you called Joshua to exhibit and which is so often found in the lives of Chinese believers. Your word and your Spirit call to me and let me know that I can live bravely. Your love compels me not to dwell on the obstacles or opposition, not to dwell on my own weakness or inability, but to focus on the needs and your willingness to empower me to meet them. I can move forward with confidence regardless of the circumstances because I know that you are with me. And Lord, look upon the Chinese church. Remember their suffering, their hardships, and grant them strength. Continue to anoint them and grant them courage. Set my heart on fire with a passion for the kingdom like theirs so that I too might share the life of Christ with others.

---

[2] Lu Xiaomin, *Sounds of the Heart*, 472 (Song #420).

Meditation #11:
An Amazing Christmas

And there were shepherds living out in the fields nearby, keeping watch over their flocks at night. An angel of the Lord appeared to them, and the glory of the Lord shone around them, and they were terrified. But the angel said to them, 'Do not be afraid. I bring you good news of great joy that will be for all the people. Today in the town of David a Saviour has been born to you; he is Christ the Lord. This will be a sign to you: You will find a baby wrapped in cloths and lying in a manger.' …

So they hurried off and found Mary and Joseph, and the baby, who was lying in the manger. When they had seen him, they spread the word concerning what had been told them about this child, and all who heard it were amazed at what the shepherds said to them (Lk. 2:8–12, 16–18).

Then they called them in again and commanded them not to speak or teach at all in the name of Jesus. But Peter and John replied, 'Judge for yourselves whether it is right in God's sight to obey you rather than God. For we cannot help speaking about what we have seen and heard' (Acts 4:18–20).

Our Chinese friends continue to amaze and encourage us with their boldness for Christ. Although the threat of persecution is ever-present and real, the attitude of our Chinese friends is reminiscent of that of Peter and John in

Acts 4:19–20. When commanded by the authorities not to speak of Jesus, Peter and John replied, 'Judge for yourselves whether it is right in God's sight to obey you rather than God. For we cannot help speaking about what we have seen and heard.' Our Chinese friends are responding to the threat of government persecution in a similar manner. When we received news that local officials were planning to crack-down on house churches in our region, I asked a local believer how he felt we should respond. He said that we should continue to use wisdom, but that we must not stop meeting, preaching and witnessing. How could we do otherwise? For him, like Peter and John, to stop speaking about Jesus was simply not an option. The following story illustrates this boldness.

Christmas in China offers wonderful opportunities to share the love of Christ. So I was not surprised when our house church friends suggested that we have a Christmas party. It was a great idea. We would invite our non-Christian friends to the party and share Christian songs and testimonies with them. All this seemed reasonable, but I was not prepared for what followed.

The team in charge of finding a suitable location selected a large meeting room in a hotel in our city. The size of the room shocked me and in the wake of news of a crack-down, I marvelled at their boldness. Then the plans for the programme grew to include not only Christian songs and testimonies, but a skit of the prodigal son and an evangelistic message complete with a public call for commitment to Christ. I must admit I was a little apprehensive, but glad for the vision of the church members. As we all worked together preparing for the party, the Lord knit our hearts together and a new sense of unity and purpose permeated the church.

The night of the party came, just two days before Christmas. I arrived early to help with last minute preparations, and the auditorium quickly filled up. With over 150 people packed into the room, the programme began. A time of singing was followed by two testimonies from church members. Then came the skit, which was a wonderful Chinese adaptation of the parable. Finally, the gospel was presented and a call to follow Christ was given. After a time of prayer many came forward and shared that they had committed their lives to Christ. That night over 20 people made decisions to follow Christ. It was an amazing Christmas, one that I will not soon forget.

Lord, I give you thanks, for although you are truly the King of kings, you chose to reveal yourself to the lowly, the shepherds, people like me. Kings and rulers trembled, but shepherds rejoiced. And so it is today. Thank you for coming, for seeking me out and bringing me life. I pray that I might be a herald like the shepherds, for I too am a witness of your coming. In the midst of opposition, enable me to respond, 'I cannot help but speak about what I have seen and heard.'

Meditation #12:
Back to Jerusalem

Then Jesus came to them and said, 'All authority in heaven and on earth has been given to me. Therefore go and make disciples of all nations, baptising them in the name of the Father and of the Son and of the Holy Spirit, and teaching them to obey everything I have commanded you. And surely I am with you always, to the very end of the age' (Mt. 28:18–20).

Not long ago I spoke with Pastor Zhou, a leader of a house church network that asked us to partner with them in establishing an underground Bible school. As we discussed what the school might look like, Pastor Zhou emphasized that they wanted a strong missions component in the curriculum. I thought this was terrific, but assumed that he was largely interested in preparing their students for cross-cultural ministry within the borders of China. But as he explained further, I quickly saw that I had underestimated their vision. Pastor Zhou stated that they felt God had called the Chinese church 'to take the gospel back to Jerusalem'. He noted that the gospel was first shared in Jerusalem. And then, for the most part, the gospel was taken westward to Europe and then North America. Finally, missionaries brought the gospel to China. Now, Pastor Zhou affirmed, the Chinese church believes that they have been called by God to take the gospel back to Jerusalem. 'We believe that God wants us to send missionaries to Pakistan, Iran, Afghanistan and on to Jerusalem.' He looked at my white, American face and said, 'It would be difficult for you to go there, but we Chinese have a long history of dealings with these peoples and nations. We can fit in easily. God is calling us to go.' Back to Jerusalem – what a wonderful vision!

Lord, I marvel at the majesty and wonder of your redemptive plan. Your gospel will go forward and it will be preached to those in every nation. I am filled with joy as I see that you are raising up missionaries in many lands and many nations. Enable these anointed evangelists to take the gospel to peoples and cultures that are not familiar. Help them cross high mountains and deep streams. Allow them to travel to distant places so they may boldly bear witness to your name. And raise up many from China. I give you thanks for the vision that you are placing within the hearts of Chinese Christians. I pray that you would strengthen them for this awesome task. As they journey to Jerusalem, may the promise of your abiding presence be fulfilled powerfully in their lives. And let me too have a part in this awesome task.

Meditation #13:
Bold Witness

'When you are brought before synagogues, rulers and authorities, do not worry about how you will defend yourselves or what you will say, for the Holy Spirit will teach you at that time what you should say' (Lk. 12:11–12).

Then Peter, filled with the Holy Spirit, said to them: 'Rulers and elders of the people! If we are being called to account today for an act of kindness shown to a cripple and are asked how he was healed, then know this, you and all the people of Israel: It is by the name of Jesus Christ of Nazareth, whom you crucified but whom God raised from the dead, that this man stands before you healed. He is

'"the stone you builders rejected,
    which has become the capstone."'
Salvation is found in no one else, for there is no other name under heaven given to men by which we must be saved.'

When they saw the courage of Peter and John and realized that they were unschooled, ordinary men, they were astonished and they took note that these men had been with Jesus (Acts 4:8–13).

Sister Yang, a tiny young lady in her mid-thirties, is a Communist Party member and an administrator at a university in a large city. One night during a Bible study she shared her testimony.

Sister Yang had been very sick and near death. She started practising *Qi gong* in the hope of gaining back her strength. Yet she saw no improvement. However, as a result of the prayers and witness of Christian friends, she was healed and committed her life to Christ. She was very excited and began to share her testimony with some of the students at the university. She also gave several students Bibles.

Word of this got back to the Communist Party leaders at the university. The leaders called her in. Two large men were present and they began to discuss the matter with her. They asked her, 'What is all this talk about Jesus?' They then ridiculed Christianity as a superstition. They told her that as a Communist Party member she could not be a Christian. They also emphasized that she should stop attending the house church meetings. Finally, after they felt sure this tiny young lady was sufficiently intimidated, they said to her, 'You have two roads before you: one is the road of the Communist Party; the other is the road of Jesus. Which one will you choose?'

Without hesitation, she answered, 'You can take away my party membership, but I cannot live without Jesus.'

Amazed at her boldness, I asked, 'What did they say?'

Sister Yang replied, 'They were shocked and didn't know what to say. Finally, they mumbled, "Well, you must pay your party dues!" and left me alone.'

Lord, I thank you for the promise of assistance you give. When I find myself facing opposition, I know that your Holy Spirit is there to give me strength and to direct me. I rejoice because I know that you will give me the power and the words I need so that I may be the witness that you have called me to be. Help me be bold and courageous, like the Chinese sister whom I have just read about. Enable me to live in such a way that people will notice that I too have been with Jesus.

Meditation #14:
'Filling in' for a
Communist Party Member

As Jesus went on from there, he saw a man named Matthew sitting at the tax collector's booth. 'Follow me,' he told him, and Matthew got up and followed him.

While Jesus was having dinner at Matthew's house, many tax collectors and 'sinners' came and ate with him and his disciples. When the Pharisees saw this, they asked his disciples, 'Why does your teacher eat with tax collectors and "sinners"?'

On hearing this, Jesus said, 'It is not the healthy who need a doctor, but the sick. But go and learn what this means: "I desire mercy, not sacrifice." For I have not come to call the righteous, but sinners' (Mt. 9:9–13).

One Saturday morning I attended the house church meeting at Brother Zhang's place. Brother Zhang, a close friend, had asked me to 'fill in' for him and preach to the small gathering. You see, Brother Zhang could not attend the meeting because he, as a Communist Party member, had to vote in an election for a Communist Party position (he mentioned that he knew none of the names of the many people listed on the ballot). There are now ten Communist Party members who have become Christians in this particular small network of house churches.

On this day about 12 adults had gathered to worship, including a man in his mid-thirties who was attending for the first time. Later, I learnt that this man had been introduced to the church leaders by a friend. However, when the man walked into the room where we had gathered, I must admit my imagination ran wild and I wondered if he was a government 'plant'. My fears were clearly misguided and the service went forward without any difficulties. It was a wonderful time of prayer, worship, testimonies and preaching. At the end of the service, Sister Zhang asked the man what he thought about the meeting and the message. The man shared that he was hungry to know God and intrigued by the message. He wanted to know more. I had the joy of sharing the gospel with him, right there in front of the group, and of leading him in the sinner's prayer. Afterwards we all gathered round, laid hands on him, and prayed a prayer of blessing and dedication for him. It was a marvellous way to welcome him into the body of Christ. It was moving to see this man's hunger. He has a wife and young daughter. He asked if he might borrow a book of Christian songs so that he might share the lyrics and the music with his family.

Lord, how thankful I am that you have come to call and to save sinners. I give you thanks for I know that although I was very much like Matthew, a sinner, to me you also called out, 'Follow me'. And Lord, I praise you, for you are still calling and saving sinners. As I read about Communist Party members and others, like the young man in the story above, who are now following you, I am reminded that you look upon the heart and are not blinded by mere outward appearances. I am reminded that you see not what we are, but what we might be through the power of your love. Lord, help me to be mindful of this. Help me to treat others with mercy, as you have treated me.

Meditation #15:
More Blessed to Give

'Do not store up for yourselves treasures on earth, where moth and rust destroy, and where thieves break in and steal. But store up for yourselves treasures in heaven, where moth and rust do not destroy, and where thieves do not break in and steal. For where your treasure is, there your heart will be also. ...

'No-one can serve two masters. Either he will hate the one and love the other, or he will be devoted to the one and despise the other. You cannot serve both God and Money' (Mt. 6:19–21, 24).

'In everything I did, I showed you that by this kind of hard work we must help the weak, remembering the words the Lord Jesus himself said: "It is more blessed to give than to receive"' (Acts 20:35).

Some time ago a Chinese pastor and I travelled to a rural area to meet with local Christians there. We stayed at a local guesthouse. The room was a real bargain. Early the next morning we set out on foot for a minority village. It was a steep and at times harrowing climb (two hours up and, coming back a safer way, five hours down). When we arrived we had a wonderful time of fellowship and worship in the church. We then examined a water project that we had sponsored. The village was desperately poor and had been suffering from an acute water shortage.

With our aid, the church had built a water cistern and 3,300 metres of pipe had been laid, effectively solving their water problem.

We had agreed to help the church build this desperately needed water system with the understanding that when they collected their next harvest, they in turn would help us help another village. I was pleased to see that the church people of the village were eager to fulfil their part of the agreement. They suggested we help a nearby village that was suffering with a similar water problem. This village had already raised almost 40 per cent of the funds they needed. With the assistance of the first village, which the church people freely gave, we were able to help the church in this second village buy the needed materials for their water system. It was so good to see the spirit of giving and cooperation exhibited in this project.

We hiked home, passing through another very poor village. As we entered it we found four ladies, a man and a young girl carrying heavy loads of roof tiles some distance on their backs. They were believers helping to build a new church. It was a moving sight to see the villagers, especially the young girl, working so hard. Partnering together with people like these, so eager to give of themselves for others and the cause of Christ, reminded me that indeed it is more blessed to give.

Lord, I praise you because you are the Supreme Giver. You delight to give good gifts and you long to enable me to do likewise. Help me focus on those things, those pursuits, which have eternal value. Give me wisdom so that I might value that which cannot be stolen and that which will not tarnish with time. Above all, enable me, in accordance with your will, to cultivate a generous heart and spirit, one that is eager to give.

Meditation #16:
The Testimony of a
Young Chinese Evangelist

Having brought the apostles, they made them appear before the Sanhedrin to be questioned by the high priest. 'We gave you strict orders not to teach in this name,' he said. 'Yet you have filled Jerusalem with your teaching and are determined to make us guilty of this man's blood.'

Peter and the other apostles replied: 'We must obey God rather than men! The God of our fathers raised Jesus from the dead – whom you had killed by hanging him on a tree. God exalted him to his own right hand as Prince and Saviour that he might give repentance and forgiveness of sins to Israel. We are witnesses of these things, and so is the Holy Spirit, whom God has given to those who obey him' (Acts 5:27–32).

Sister Li, a good friend, shared her testimony in our regular Monday prayer meeting. She described how she came to the Lord through her mother's witness and the Lord's healing touch on her life. When she was 18 years old she began to go out and preach in outlying villages.

One day Sister Li went with a teacher and another Christian brother to encourage a group of believers in a remote village in the mountains. Her ministry was to teach the local believers some new Christian songs. The police were tipped off by a TSPM church member and the three evangelists, including 18-year-old Sister Li, were arrested and taken to the local police station. The officer in charge had her brought into his office. He tried to intimidate her by placing a gun and handcuffs on his desk. He then asked her if she had been teaching the village people new songs. 'Yes,' she answered. The police officer asked her what her songs were about, so she started to sing. The song went like this: 'I have a question, who made the universe and all that is in it?' She stopped at this point.

The officer rather anxiously asked her, 'Continue, what is the answer?'

So she continued singing, 'You may ask me who? The answer is that there is a God in heaven who has created all things; he has created you and he has created me.'

The officer cried out, but now laughing, 'You're trying to evangelize me.' Sister Li said that she was a good citizen and was simply answering his question.

The three evangelists were placed in prison. Sister Li was the youngest person in the prison. They were placed in a small room with 12 other inmates. One lady in particular was very rude to Sister Li. Her boyfriend had stolen some gold from the jewellery factory where she worked, had promptly run off, and left her to take the blame. She was very bitter. All day long she would play cards by herself. Sister Li offered to play cards with her in an attempt to build a relationship. Lit first the lady was reluctant, but Sister Li finally won her over. As they played, Sister Li told her that her greatest joy in life was Jesus. She said that Jesus was her best friend. When the lady heard this she burst into tears. She had been betrayed by her boyfriend and felt totally alone. As Sister Li spoke the cell became quiet – the others were now listening too. Sister Li shared the good news of Jesus' love with that lady in the cell. She, along with a number of the other inmates, responded and became Christians.

The old routines in the prison changed. Now, after eating breakfast, they would sing songs and study the Bible. This went on for several days. The guards could hear the singing and the preaching, so one day the chief officer called Sister Li into his office and said to her, 'Your songs are very nice, but you cannot preach. This is not a church, it's a prison.'

Sister Li answered, 'We cannot sing, if we cannot preach.' He told her not to preach or sing anymore. But she and the others continued to do so.

Several prisoners were so changed that they were released a short time later. Sister Li wondered, 'Lord, why do they get to go free, but I have to stay here.' Finally after 20 days, Sister Li was also released. As the police officer escorted her to the local bus station, he shared with her that his mother was a Christian. He indicated that Sister Li and her songs had made a big impact on his life.

Lord, I acknowledge that you are indeed the Saviour and that forgiveness of sins is found only in you. I thank you for the wonder of your sacrificial death and the power of your resurrection. Your death, through faith, provides access; your resurrection power enables me to change. And I rejoice because now I am able to call you my friend. Enable me to 'fill' my town, my city, with the message of your love. Help me, through the power of the Holy Spirit, to be a witness for you.

Meditation #17:
The Gracious Gift

For I received from the Lord what I also passed on to you:
The Lord Jesus, on the night he was betrayed, took bread,
and when he had given thanks, he broke it and said, 'This is
my body, which is for you; do this in remembrance of me.'
In the same way, after supper he took the cup, saying, 'This
cup is the new covenant in my blood; do this, whenever you
drink it, in remembrance of me.' For whenever you eat this
bread and drink this cup, you proclaim the Lord's death
until he comes (1 Cor. 11:23–26).

I arrived early, yet found the church already packed with
people. The sanctuary was filled to capacity; even its
aisles were clogged with people on wicker stools. I made
my way up the staircase leading to the balcony, but soon
found that every available seat had been taken. So I sat
down on a step halfway up the staircase. People crowded
in around me. None of us could see into the sanctuary,
but we could hear the sounds of worship.

It was communion Sunday, and soon the emblems
were being passed out. As a container of small cups
reached the staircase, it became apparent that there
would not be enough for everyone. A group of ten or
more – myself included – stared at the last cup. The man
who held it looked around, wondering what to do. When
he spotted me – a foreigner – he placed the cup in my
hand. There I stood in the midst of a sea of eager faces, the

only one holding this powerful symbol of God's grace. I will not soon forget that moment, the graciousness of the Giver/giver, the way the event mirrored a larger reality. The faces of those around me, those without a cup, reminded me why I had come to China.

Lord, I worship you for you alone are worthy of worship. I look back and remember how you died for me and so enabled me to truly live. I look forward and rejoice for I know that you are coming to establish your kingdom in its fullness. And today, I ask that you would help me proclaim in word and deed your greatness and love. Lord, I know that there are many who stand unable to grasp the cup, unable to receive the gift. Help me be a giver today.

Meditation #18:
Spiritual Darkness in China

For there is no difference between Jew and Gentile – the same Lord is Lord of all and richly blesses all who call on him, for, 'Everyone who calls on the name of the Lord will be saved.'

How, then, can they call on the one they have not believed in? And how can they believe in the one of whom they have not heard? And how can they hear without someone preaching to them? And how can they preach unless they are sent? As it is written, 'How beautiful are the feet of those who bring good news!' (Rom. 10:12–15).

Recent statistics indicate that the revival in China has produced the fastest growing church in the world. Yet, in spite of this miraculous growth, there are still many areas in China where the gospel is virtually unknown. It is not unusual to find regions of deep spiritual darkness adjacent to communities with thriving churches. A number of factors have contributed to this unusual mixture of spiritual vitality and spiritual poverty: the restrictions (which often vary from region to region) imposed upon the church by a Marxist government, the relative immobility of a largely peasant society, the sheer vastness of the country, and the lingering strength of traditional religions are but a few. So, while churches continue to grow, the sobering fact remains: China is, in many regions, a land of intense spiritual darkness.

The depth of China's spiritual darkness is illustrated in several encounters with individual Chinese. Several years ago I travelled in a remote, mountainous region of China. After hiking down the side of a mountain, I entered a beautiful village that was full of small huts, excited children and clacking chickens. After speaking with several elderly villagers, I noticed the village temple. Entering the temple compound, I met the religious leader of the village. His duties included caring for the temple and passing on the religious traditions of the community encoded in an ancient script. After briefly getting acquainted, I directed the conversation towards spiritual matters, stating, 'Your temple is beautiful, but I am a Christian.' The man looked puzzled. I repeated the words. Again, the man showed no signs of comprehension. 'Haven't you heard of Christianity?' I asked. He shook his head, indicating he had not. 'Haven't you heard of Jesus Christ?' I asked.

With a vacant look in his eyes, he answered, 'No, I have not yet heard.'

The character of the spiritual darkness in the cities is often quite different from that of the rural regions. Once, I spoke with a young waitress in a local restaurant. She initiated the conversation and spoke in English, obviously eager to try out her language skills. When she learnt that I was a teacher, she quickly asked what subjects I taught. I responded, 'History and theology.' (Although due to government restrictions we must be cautious concerning how we present ourselves to strangers, I felt this was an appropriate response.) She understood 'history', but struggled with 'theology'. Finally, a look of comprehension flashed across her eyes and in Chinese she confidently uttered the word for 'geography'. I shook my head and said, '*shen xue*' (the Chinese word for 'theology').

A shocked look covered her faced, and she gasped, 'God? You believe in God? No one believes in God anymore!' I assured her that many people do believe in God and that I happened to be one of them. The impact of years of atheistic propaganda was all too evident.

Finally, on a recent trip to a large city, I saw evidence of the strength of traditional Chinese religions, especially Buddhism, even in an urban centre. In this great city I saw a young woman, perhaps 20 years of age, prostrating herself before a Buddhist idol. Full of anguish, she prayed to the image made by human hands. It was dusk, but even in spiritual terms, the darkness seemed to engulf her.

Lord, how easily I forget that there are many people in our world who have never heard your name, people who have no opportunity to know and worship you. And the Scriptures remind us that in order for these people to believe and enter into relationship with you, they must first hear. And if they are to hear, messengers must go, they must be sent. Lord, speak to me concerning my place in your redemptive plan. What would you have me do so that others might hear? Empower me so that I might help push back the darkness in my region and in the world.

Meditation #19:
An Invisible Army

You then, my son, be strong in the grace that is in Christ Jesus. And the things you have heard me say in the presence of many witnesses entrust to reliable men who will also be qualified to teach others. Endure hardship with us like a good soldier of Christ Jesus. No-one serving as a soldier gets involved in civilian affairs – he wants to please his commanding officer. …

Remember Jesus Christ, raised from the dead, descended from David. This is my gospel, for which I am suffering even to the point of being chained like a criminal. But God's word is not chained. Therefore I endure everything for the sake of the elect, that they too may obtain the salvation that is in Christ Jesus, with eternal glory (2 Tim. 2:1–4, 8–10).

We Do Not Fear Strong Wind and Rain

We do not fear strong wind and rain
  For the one with us is Jehovah
We do not fear strong wind and rain
  For the one with us is greater than ten thousand
We will not cast our nets in the narrow, shallow stream
  Nor will we cast our nets in the tranquil lake
Small trees survive violent winds and savage rain
  They grow into tall trees that reach to heaven.[1]

---

[1] Lu Xiaomin, *Sounds of the Heart*, 455 (Song #404).

We are an Invisible ArWe are an invisible army
    We are evangelists without names
If God helps us, who can stand against us?
    'Charge forward' is our battle cry
The blood of martyrs spilled over thousands of years,
    Cries out to those of us who follow
The throng of saints over thousands of years,
    In ragged clothes, drifting, yet not discouraged
On the battlefield these soldiers were tested
    In strong winds and waves these helmsmen were tried
In these last days we will face even greater trials
    So we constantly ask the Lord for His guidance.[2]

Lord, I thank you and praise you because you have called me to be a part of your vast, invisible army. I rejoice because I stand side by side with countless Chinese believers and other Christians from every nation. I ask for your guidance and strength, because I know the task is great. Enable me to exhibit a bit of the courage and stamina that animate the Chinese church. Lord, I do not want to simply cast my net in shallow streams or peaceful waters, but I want to be obedient to your calling and be willing to face difficult challenges. Help me live in a manner worthy of your calling.

---

[2] Lu Xiaomin, *Sounds of the Heart*, 585 (Song #524).

Meditation #20:
Transforming Pagan Rituals

While Paul was waiting for them in Athens, he was greatly distressed to see that the city was full of idols. So he reasoned in the synagogue with the Jews and the God-fearing Greeks, as well as in the market-place day by day with those who happened to be there. ...

Paul then stood up in the meeting of the Areopagus and said: 'Men of Athens! I see that in every way you are very religious. For as I walked around and looked carefully at your objects of worship, I even found an altar with this inscription: TO AN UNKNOWN GOD. Now what you worship as something unknown I am going to proclaim to you.

'The God who made the world and everything in it is the Lord of heaven and earth and does not live in temples built by hands. And he is not served by human hands, as if he needed anything, because he himself gives all men life and breath and everything else. From one man he made every nation of men, that they should inhabit the whole earth; and he determined the times set for them and the exact places where they should live. God did this so that men would seek him and perhaps reach out for him and find him, though he is not far from each one of us. "For in him we live and move and have our being." As some of your own poets have said, "We are his offspring"' (Acts 17:16–17, 22–28).

One bright day I hiked up into the mountains with a Chinese Christian friend, his uncle and the leader of the village. We met a host of my friend's relatives at their ancestral burial grounds high in the mountains. There we witnessed a number of pagan rituals that prefaced a festive picnic. The centuries-old rituals included three ceremonies: first, food was offered on a small altar to the mountain god; second, family members bowed down before the family ancestral tablet; and third, each family member bowed down before the individual graves of their ancestors. I, along with my friend, did not participate in these ceremonies and we requested that we be given food not offered to the mountain god. This was all accepted well and we were able to establish many meaningful relationships amid the food and festivities.

It was exciting to talk with my friend about the ceremonies and ask how they might be transformed and given new Christian content. We agreed that the initial ceremony was the key: could this be transformed so as to focus on the creator, the one true God who has revealed himself in Jesus Christ? Could the contributions of past ancestors, especially as a Christian heritage emerges, be reaffirmed in a way that would actually bear witness to Christ and Christian values? It was exciting to speak of these customs and to consider how Christ might be honoured through their transformation. As family members become Christians, I pray and believe this will indeed happen.

Lord, I acknowledge that you do not inhabit the shrines or altars that we have erected to contain your presence. You are not limited to sacred places or manipulated by special rituals. You do not need our assistance or service. You are the Creator and all things exist by your power and in accordance with your will. And yet, incredibly, you are not far off. Oh, I rejoice, because you are near. And you love to be acknowledged and worshipped by me. You delight to have fellowship with me, one whom you have created. Lord, help me worship you and delight to be with you as I should. Enable me to help others also become worshippers of you.

Meditation #21:
Strong Measures

Dear friends, do not be surprised at the painful trial you are suffering, as though something strange were happening to you. But rejoice that you participate in the sufferings of Christ, so that you may be overjoyed when his glory is revealed. If you are insulted because of the name of Christ, you are blessed, for the Spirit of glory and of God rests on you. If you suffer, it should not be as a murderer or thief or any other kind of criminal, or even as a meddler. However, if you suffer as a Christian, do not be ashamed, but praise God that you bear that name (1 Pet. 4:12–16).

Not long ago I ran across a copy of the 30 June 1998 edition of the *Hong He County Newspaper*. Hong He (which means 'Red River') is a county in Yunnan Province, notorious for its hard-line stance against Christians.

This article details the manner in which Christians have been persecuted there. It also illustrates the complexity of the situation in China. Although some areas in China are relatively free of government interference, in other areas, such as Hong He County, no churches are tolerated and the persecution of Christians is intense. I have translated the article and offer a few excerpts.

Our County's Lawful Efforts to Punish Illegal Religious Activity in Luo En Township Meet with Initial Success

In order to maintain public order ... our county has adopted strong measures. ... In recent years in various parts of our county, especially in the remote mountain regions inhabited by minority groups, a group of illegal religious organizations which violate the spirit of socialism and disrupt the construction of civilization have appeared. ... The religious groups active in Luo En township have not received permission from the appropriate government department nor have they received the approval of recognized religious bodies. [Note: Christians have tried to register their churches, but have been denied.] A few lawless persons cloaked in religious garb and waving the banner of Christianity have, without authorization, established religious organizations and engaged in illegal religious activity. These people first seek to influence a family, then the members of the clan, and finally the extended family and their friends. They then reach out to influence the entire village and the outlying area. These methods have had a snowball effect and enabled them to form a network comprised of large groups, which meet together and which are also divided up into smaller groups. This network's influence extends to six administrative villages in Luo En (Niang Zong, Duo Jiao, Cao Guo, Pu Mi, Ci Nong, and La Bo), including 22 natural villages. A total of 18 meeting points have been utilized by the 235 families and 425 people engaged in these illegal religious activities. ...

At 2:00 am, early on the morning of the 13th, the work group [98 comrades] separated into three groups and boldly and powerfully launched their attack, rushing towards their prearranged objectives: the villages of Suo Ma, Yang Pu, and Tai An. Two believers in Suo Ma village, Li Hu Gan and Li Hu Liu, grabbed a knife and attempted to block the work group from carrying out their official business. These men were lawfully arrested. [Note: local believers indicate that the two men did not resist the officials once they realized they were government representatives.] At Yang Pu village in the home of the religious ringleader Chen Wen Qing, the work group discovered and seized over 20 illegal evangelistic books, including *A Complete Bible (Old and New Testaments)*, *The Three-Self According to Scripture*, *Hymns of Praise*, and *A Commentary on First Corinthians*. The first phase of the enforcement work, meticulously directed by the county Communist Party Committee and government, dealt the ringleaders propagating religion a severe blow ... [and] prepared the way for the next step. [End of article.]

Lord, I confess that I am weak and often lack courage. The very thought of persecution makes me shudder. And yet I know that persecution is a reality that many Christians around the world face daily. It is not something strange or unusual. It was the common experience of the early church and it is routinely experienced by believers in China and many other places in the world. Strengthen me so that if persecution comes, I might it embrace it gladly, knowing that I am so treated because I bear your name. And help me identify with and pray for my Christian brothers and sisters who are persecuted. I pray especially for the believers in Hong He County. I pray that you would bless and encourage them. Continue to strengthen them and give them boldness. Fill them with the hope that only you can give. I pray also that you might move the hearts of the government leaders there. Help them see your love and righteousness in the lives of the Christians that they mistreat. May these leaders repent, change their ways and turn to you.

Meditation #22:
The Unreached Mosuo

He came and took the scroll from the right hand of him who sat on the throne. And when he had taken it, the four living creatures and the twenty-four elders fell down before the Lamb. Each one had a harp and they were holding golden bowls full of incense, which are the prayers of the saints. And they sang a new song:

'You are worthy to take the scroll
    and to open its seals,
because you were slain,
    and with your blood you purchased men for God
    from every tribe and language and people and nation.
You have made them to be a kingdom and priests to serve
    our God,
    and they will reign on the earth.'

Then I looked and heard the voice of many angels, numbering thousands upon thousands, and ten thousand times ten thousand. They encircled the throne and the living creatures and the elders. In a loud voice they sang:

'Worthy is the Lamb, who was slain,
to receive power and wealth and wisdom and strength
and honour and glory and praise!' (Rev. 5:7–12).

The Mosuo people have lived for centuries by the pristine, crystal-clear waters of Lu Gu Lake. It took the driver of the small van we rented ten hours to navigate the bumpy and treacherous mountain roads that bind Lu Gu Lake to the town where we had stayed. When we arrived, we were immediately struck by the beauty of the area and the Mosuo villages, both relatively untouched by modern development. One of the Mosuo houses we visited was over 400 years old, and yet the inhabitants indicated that they had only received electricity the previous year.

In spite of the beauty of their land, the Mosuo have significant spiritual and social needs. One village we visited was 20 kilometres from the nearest doctor. Educational opportunities are also very limited: the local primary school has a 30–40 per cent drop-out rate because the students must travel so far.

Mosuo society is matriarchal, and this distinctive feature of their culture was very evident. When we ate lunch in one home, the great grandmother, grandmother, mother and daughter – four generations of women – were all present, but no men were to be found. In fact, I was told that the Mosuo language does not even have a word for 'father'. Marriage customs are also lax. Most Mosuo do not marry until after their first child is born.

A 16-year-old young man named Er Qi helped paddle us across a portion of Lu Gu Lake in a canoe hewn out of a single, large log. With a mischievous grin, Er Qi noted that he was free to have many 'girlfriends'. I told Er Qi that I was a Christian and that we Christians only have one wife. Nodding to my wife, I emphasized that I was very satisfied with one wife. This led to a discussion of Christianity. Er Qi's first comment was: 'You Christians don't eat and then die, right?' Obviously there were some misconceptions to dispel and a lot of ground to cover.

As I shared the gospel with Er Qi, things got really interesting. Mosuo religious beliefs have been largely shaped by Tibetan Buddhism and related forms of spiritism. There are no Christian churches among the Mosuo and they are considered unreached. So, when Er Qi mentioned that he knew two Mosuo Christians, I was very surprised. Two years ago, he said, there was a Mosuo couple who became followers of Christ. However, they were arrested by the local police and sent to prison. Er Qi clearly felt the couple had been arrested because they were Christians.

When I heard these words I could not help but think of all the obstacles which kept the Mosuo from hearing and responding to the gospel – their isolation, their spiritism, the government restrictions – the difficulties seemed so large. But then I thought of some of the other minority groups and what God had done in their midst. I was reminded afresh of God's power to transform lives and to break through seemingly insurmountable obstacles. I began to pray that God would send missionaries to the Mosuo.

This experience took place about seven years ago. Just this past month several Chinese friends travelled to the area and shared the gospel with the Mosuo. I was very excited to learn that as a result of their ministry, several Mosuo became followers of Jesus.

Lord, you alone are worthy of my worship. I praise you because with your blood you have 'purchased', you have redeemed, people from every tribe and every language and every nation, men and women from every people group, including the Mosuo. I marvel at your awesome power and the depth of your love. I rejoice because even now you are reaching out, breaking through every conceivable barrier, and calling people from previously unreached groups to worship you. Lord, I pray that you would bless these new Mosuo believers and those that minister among this group. Help them demonstrate your love and righteousness in such a way that many others would follow in their footsteps. Empower their witness. Stretch out your hand and perform signs and wonders in their midst. I pray that a revival would stir this people and bring transformation.

Lord, I also acknowledge that although you delight to use me, sometimes I have been slow to hear your voice and slow to obey. Oh, Lord, help me see the world and its needs as you see them. Enable me to respond as I should. Use me, Lord, use me!

Meditation #23:
Those Who Prepared the Way

How beautiful on the mountains
   are the feet of those who bring good news,
who proclaim peace,
   who bring good tidings,
   who proclaim salvation,
who say to Zion,
   'Your God reigns!'
Listen! Your watchmen lift up their voices;
   together they shout for joy.
When the LORD returns to Zion,
   they will see it with their own eyes.
Burst into songs of joy together,
   you ruins of Jerusalem,
for the LORD has comforted his people,
   he has redeemed Jerusalem.
The LORD will lay bare his holy arm
   in the sight of all the nations,
and all the ends of the earth will see
   the salvation of our God (Is. 52:7–10).

Several years ago I had the privilege of preaching in a remote Lisu village. Later that same day, in another Lisu church, my colleagues and I met with local believers for a late-night service, sharing testimonies and singing songs of praise. We were all overwhelmed with the hospitality and kindness shown to us. It quickly became apparent why we were treated with such respect. In both services, church leaders noted how a century ago missionaries from the West had brought the gospel to their people. One of these early missionaries, James Fraser, provided the Lisu people with a written script and translated the Bible into their language. Other missionaries, perhaps less well-known, served faithfully among the Lisu until the Communist takeover. One Lisu leader, speaking of these early missionaries, stated, 'We have not forgotten one missionary who came and served here.'

Many of the believers we met indicated that we were the first western missionaries they had seen. They had heard the stories of how the gospel had come to their people, but they personally had not met any missionaries. I was inspired by the impact of the service and the sacrifice of these early pioneers. Most of all, however, my colleagues and I were humbled to learn that we were somehow identified with them and thus treated with such deference. The words of Isaiah 52:7 were validated in our hearts in a fresh way: 'How beautiful on the mountains are the feet of those who bring good news.' We were truly blessed. Our God truly reigns.

Lord, I bless your name for you are revealing your strength and love to the nations. The ends of the earth shall see your salvation. People from every tribe and nation shall together worship you. And Lord, I give you thanks for the way you have moved godly men and women in the past to sacrifice much so that they might serve others in your name. I think of people like James Fraser and I am moved. I am so thankful for the countless men and women who, at great cost, have prepared the way. I now reap the blessings that come from the seeds which they sowed many years ago. Thank you Lord for this incredible heritage and example. Help me leave a legacy of blessing in your name.

Meditation #24:
Relentless Grace

He told them another parable: 'The kingdom of heaven is like a mustard seed, which a man took and planted in his field. Though it is the smallest of all your seeds, yet when it grows, it is the largest of garden plants and becomes a tree, so that the birds of the air come and perch in its branches' (Mt. 13:31–32).

In December 2002 I participated in a wonderful Christmas party put on by a house church group that I had encouraged and watched develop over the previous four years. The Christmas programme symbolized how much the church had developed over this short period of time. The group rented a movie theatre for the event and over 800 people attended. The theatre was so packed that the church leaders asked some of the believers to give up their seats so that the many visitors could be accommodated. The programme was wonderful – a tremendous mix of music (various styles ranging from a choir to human video), drama, testimony and preaching. After it was over, around 100 people who had committed their lives to Christ that evening remained to receive instruction in the faith. I spoke with a young professor from a local school who had become a follower of Jesus that evening. He spoke with genuine excitement about his experience and this new direction for his life.

The programme represented a major leap forward from the very humble beginnings of the church. Gone were the desperate days of the early years when even I was asked to sing. The quality had been truly amazing.

It was especially encouraging to see so many people who, over the years, had been touched through the ministry of the church. One man who shared his testimony in the programme came to faith at the first Christmas programme three years ago. He is now an incredibly faithful brother and a gifted minister. His testimony was deeply moving. Another man, a Communist Party member, who was prominent in the programme came up afterwards and we reminisced about how a little over two years ago he and his wife came to faith. I still remember how, after attending our services several times, he had wrestled with the possible cost of following Christ. He knew that faith in Christ was a contradiction for a Communist Party member. Nevertheless, one evening he made the decision to follow Christ, regardless of the cost. Shortly after this profession of faith he was baptized. There were many others whom I saw that night. Each one represented a story of God's grace powerfully at work in this particular house church.

It made me think of the parable of the mustard seed (Mt. 13:31–32). God's kingdom is indeed very much like this tiny seed that grows, gradually but relentlessly, into a large plant that towers over the rest of the garden. So also the kingdom, from something seemingly insignificant and very much unnoticed, it grows in unstoppable fashion until we finally see its true significance in the lives of people. This particular house church and the lives that it represents bears witness to the unstoppable, relentless power of the kingdom of God at work in China.

Lord, I acknowledge that at times I become discouraged, and in those moments the world appears to be controlled by dark, powerful forces. I long to see, in very tangible and visible ways, the triumph of your kingdom here and now. And when I fail to see corrupt rulers brought down, the poor cared for and sinners transformed, I become impatient. And so, Lord, give me eyes to see the realities around me. Enable me to understand the significance of small beginnings. Allow me to perceive the impact that one transformed life will make. Help me grasp the awesome depth of your love and the incomparable wisdom of your redemptive plan. Lord, as my eyes are opened, I stand in awe before your unstoppable, relentless grace.

Meditation #25:
Tibetan Mist

Amos' oracle includes this description of coming judgement:

'The days are coming,' declares the Sovereign LORD,
  'when I will send a famine through the land –
not a famine of food or a thirst for water,
  but a famine of hearing the words of the LORD.
Men will stagger from sea to sea
  and wander from north to east,
searching for the word of the LORD,
  but they will not find it' (Amos 8:11–12).

However, with his last words, Amos speaks of the restoration that will come:

'In that day I will restore David's fallen tent.
I will repair its broken places,
  restore its ruins,
  and build it as it used to be,
so that they may possess the remnant of Edom
  and all the nations that bear my name,'
    declares the LORD,
      who will do these things.
'The days are coming,' declares the LORD,
'when the reaper will be overtaken by the ploughman
  and the planter by the one treading grapes.

New wine will drip from the mountains
   and flow from all the hills.
I will bring back my exiled people Israel;
   they will rebuild the ruined cities and live in them.
They will plant vineyards and drink their wine;
   they will make gardens and eat their fruit.
I will plant Israel in their own land,
   never again to be uprooted
from the land I have given them,'

    says the LORD your God (Amos 9:11–15).

Not long ago I visited a region that is largely populated by Tibetans. This region is home to a large Tibetan lamasery. I visited the lamasery one afternoon and spoke with a number of the lamas who lived there. Four young lamas invited me into their spartan living quarters, where we drank tea and chatted. I spoke with them at length, but two aspects of our conversation were especially striking.

First, these young men, now in their late twenties, had all come to the lamasery as young boys (10–12 years old). They knew very little about the outside world or other religions. Their studies focused on the Tibetan language and scriptures and they were aware of little else. When I asked them if they had heard of Jesus, one clearly had never even heard the name and the others simply looked puzzled. Second, when I asked them about the creator and his creation, I was frequently told that my questions could only be answered in Tibetan (not in Chinese), even though they were all quite conversant in Chinese. I believe this puzzling response reflected their training, which consists almost entirely of memorization of set texts. To the lamas, the Tibetan scriptures are sacred and so they are memorized. Any deviation from the text, including translation, is difficult to contemplate. This highlighted to me the necessity of providing the Bible and other Christian literature in the Tibetan language; nothing else would be taken seriously by these men.

As I peered through the charcoal mist that filled the lama's room, I had one thought: the barriers are indeed great, but God's love and power is greater.

This experience took place about six years ago. As I write this meditation I am reminded that just two days ago I had the joy of speaking and praying with a Tibetan man in his early thirties who came to faith in Christ four months ago. He spent ten years in India studying as a Buddhist monk. He then travelled to the lamasery noted above and continued his studies. But there, through the witness of a Chinese brother, he encountered Jesus and was changed. He is now studying the Bible and, as one who speaks and writes Tibetan, he hopes to share the gospel with his people.

Lord, I know that many regions of the world are experiencing famine; not a famine of food or drink, but a famine of your word. As I think of the young monks in this Tibetan lamasery, I am reminded of this fact. But I praise your name because you are at work restoring and redeeming. You are dispelling the clouds and the mist and transforming lives. The days are coming for the Tibetans, when the reaper will be overtaken by the ploughman. New wine will flow from these high mountains. And I rejoice because even now, as I reflect on my recent meeting with this new Tibetan brother, I can see a foretaste of your great work among this people. I pray that you would enable this young man to powerfully impact his people in your name. Lord, bring a harvest where there was once only desolation.

Meditation #26:
Resilient Faith

Furious with rage, Nebuchadnezzar summoned Shadrach, Meshach and Abednego. So these men were brought before the king, and Nebuchadnezzar said to them, 'Is it true, Shadrach, Meshach and Abednego, that you do not serve my gods or worship the image of gold I have set up? Now when you hear the sound of the horn, flute, zither, lyre, harp, pipes and all kinds of music, if you are ready to fall down and worship the image I made, very good. But if you do not worship it, you will be thrown immediately into a blazing furnace. Then what god will be able to rescue you from my hand?'

Shadrach, Meshach and Abednego replied to the king, 'O Nebuchadnezzar, we do not need to defend ourselves before you in this matter. If we are thrown into the blazing furnace, the God we serve is able to save us from it, and he will rescue us from your hand, O king. But even if he does not, we want you to know, O king, that we will not serve your gods or worship the image of gold you have set up' (Dan. 3:13–18).

A few years ago I, along with several colleagues, was privileged to hold a three-day seminar in a remote Bible training centre. The seminar was attended by 75 minority students from a number of villages in this mountainous area, and stressed Bible teaching and instruction in leading worship. One friend, using her special musical gifting, taught the students how to play the guitar and electric piano, and also introduced them to many new worship songs. We all had opportunities to preach and teach.

It was a very busy, stretching and wonderful time. We remained on the small campus throughout our stay, and from morning until night were involved in teaching and preaching activities. Our days began early (since the resident rooster was perched just outside our window), and after rinsing off under a cold-water tap, we gathered together for prayer and a meal. Then the meetings began. The students were very attentive and eager to learn. Most had travelled many hours, riding dilapidated buses and walking muddy trails, to get to the school. By the end of the day we were all exhausted, ready to roll under the requisite mosquito net.

On Sunday, we ministered in a church that has a remarkable history. It all started in Burma, when the father of the current elder of the church became a Christian. Shortly after this, all of the man's livestock (cattle and chickens) died. The other villagers told him that this was due to his new-found faith in Christ (the spirits were angry) and that if he didn't recant he also would die. A local evangelist encouraged him not to do so, and his faith never wavered. In time God blessed him, and his livestock grew to twice the size of the original herd. His sons all became Christians and one migrated to the village where the church is located. This son was the first Christian in the village and, in spite of opposition, he opened his home up for Christian meetings. The church now has well over 200 committed believers (the entire village only has a population of 600) and meets five times a week for services.

The students at the school will return to provide leadership to churches such as this; many will plant new ones.

Lord, I thank you for the strong faith of this father. He did not waver when opposition and hardship came, but remained faithful to you. I rejoice in his faith, reproduced so visibly in his sons and the church that I attended. I ask that you would continue to bless this family and the churches that it has nurtured. I also ask that you would bless the Bible school and its students, many of whom will face similar tests. Enable them to demonstrate such resilient faith. Give them courage so that, even in the face of opposition, they too might declare that you alone are God and worthy of worship. Lord, help me be a person of strong faith as well. Let me not waver, but boldly and clearly declare your goodness in every situation.

Meditation #27:
Explosive Growth

Then he told them many things in parables, saying: 'A farmer went out to sow his seed. As he was scattering the seed, some fell along the path, and the birds came and ate it up. Some fell on rocky places, where it did not have much soil. It sprang up quickly, because the soil was shallow. But when the sun came up, the plants were scorched, and they withered because they had no root. Other seed fell among thorns, which grew up and choked the plants. Still other seed fell on good soil, where it produced a crop – a hundred, sixty or thirty times what was sown. He who has ears, let him hear' (Mt. 13:3–9).

One TSPM training school is located in the capital city of an eastern province. When I visited this school, it was in its second year of operation. It had four full-time faculty members and 34 students who ranged in age from 16 to 48 years old. The school's key purpose is to prepare ministers for the rapidly growing church in this province. In 1984 there were approximately 50,000 believers in the province and only six churches. At the time of my visit (1998), there were well over 600,000 believers and over 106 churches. Church leaders estimate that in this province alone 20,000–30,000 new believers are added to the church every year. The need for trained ministers is truly staggering. In 1994 there were 33 ordained pastors in the province, two-thirds of whom were over 80 years of age. It was a profound privilege to be able to teach a series of special courses in this setting. I was impressed with the students, who were keenly aware of their need for God's power and eager to do the work of the Lord. Their eagerness to study the Bible, in spite of the long hours and difficult conditions, was especially encouraging.

The stories the students and faculty told of church growth in this region were amazing. One faculty member spoke of a young lady whose home village is located in the northern part of this province, an 'unreached' region without any believers or Christian witness. The young lady travelled to Beijing to pursue college-level studies. During her time of study she heard the gospel message and became a Christian. After completing her studies in 1984, she returned to her home village. She was the only Christian in the region, but began to testify to her family and friends. As a result, by 1987 (just three years later) there were 2,000 believers in this previously unreached area. A little over ten years later, there were over 20,000 believers in this area. One of the faculty members at the school, a tiny but powerful lady, goes regularly to this area to minister since it is without pastors. She once baptized 700 believers in one day!

Many in the remote mountainous areas are coming to Christ. One young man came to the capital city to buy Bibles. When local Christians asked him how he had heard about Jesus, he indicated that it was through radio broadcasts. He said that he needed 800–900 Bibles for the believers in his area!

The faculty and students reflect the spiritual vitality of the region. They responded warmly to my teaching on the power of the Holy Spirit and sang an indigenous Chinese song based on Acts 1:8. There was a sense of excitement, commitment and joy in the school that was truly inspiring. I left in awe of what God is doing in this region and, more particularly, in this school.

Lord, I rejoice at the power of your word. I am amazed at the way in which it transforms and produces change. As I reflect on the impact this one young lady had on the lives of so many, I am greatly encouraged. I am reminded that someone shared the gospel with her in Beijing and yet that person will probably never know the process that his or her words set in motion. I too do not always know nor will I always see the fruit of my witness. And yet you are at work, seeking, wooing and finding the lost. Lord, help me not to become discouraged if some reject your message. Help me not to grow weary when I do not see visible results. Allow me to rest in the confidence that your word is powerful and that it will produce fruit: thirty, sixty, even a hundred-fold.

Meditation #28:
Standing Firm

Listen, I tell you a mystery: We will not all sleep, but we will all be changed – in a flash, in the twinkling of an eye, at the last trumpet. For the trumpet will sound, the dead will be raised imperishable, and we will be changed. For the perishable must clothe itself with the imperishable, and the mortal with immortality. When the perishable has been clothed with the imperishable, and the mortal with immortality, then the saying that is written will come true: 'Death has been swallowed up in victory.'

'Where, O death, is your victory?

Where, O death, is your sting?'

The sting of death is sin, and the power of sin is the law. But thanks be to God! He gives us the victory through our Lord Jesus Christ.

Therefore, my dear brothers, stand firm. Let nothing move you. Always give yourselves fully to the work of the Lord, because you know that your labour in the Lord is not in vain (1 Cor. 15:51–58).

China is changing rapidly. Every dimension of life here seems to be in a state of transition. The dramatic economic changes are literally altering the landscape of cities and villages. These changes are also generating new social problems, such as unemployment. In the spiritual arena, there is deep dissatisfaction with the new materialistic culture and the loss of ethical direction.

While it is true that the dramatic changes are creating new problems, it is also evident that they are creating new opportunities. This is particularly true for Christians and the church. One evidence of change is the emergence of a number of rural Bible schools nominally associated with the TSPM.

It was hard to believe that I was still in China. It seemed more like a dream than reality, too good to be true. I was standing before a group of 80 Chinese students who had come from remote villages representing six different minority groups (Lisu, Jingpo, Zhuang, Dai, Naxi and Han), exhorting them with the words of Paul: 'Stand firm. Let nothing move you. Always give yourselves fully to the work of the Lord, because you know that your labour in the Lord is not in vain' (1 Cor. 15:58).

The students and faculty at this training school are indeed 'standing firm'. In spite of obvious hardships – most of the students sleep three to a bed and live in incredibly cramped quarters – there are now 180 students who study at the school. They come every year for three to six months of training (October to March). The remainder of the year is spent either in the fields harvesting crops or in the villages preaching and teaching. The students generally study for a period of four years. After they graduate, many become pastors or evangelists in their home villages. The faculty are generally young and no less dedicated. They have no means of support other than that which is provided by their home villages and the crops they themselves can raise, yet testimonies of God's provision, power and grace abound.

This particular school began with a handful of students in a poor village in 1990. It grew rapidly, established a sister school, and is now located on a

modest campus. Although the school is very autonomous, it is not unknown to local officials.

How could this happen in China? How do Bible
schools function in a Communist country? Schools such
as this one appear to be one consequence of the changes
that are shaking China. The church in our region is
increasingly experiencing more freedom. Recently, one
friend speaking of the situation put it this way:
'Government officials no longer have time to persecute
Christians. They are too busy trying to make money!'
Although the situation varies from county to county,
local officials now tend to be preoccupied with other
matters. This change is borne out by the experiences of
high concentrations of believers, particularly in minority
areas. This has created wonderful new opportunities for
us and for our Chinese Christian friends.

Lord, I give you thanks for the hope that you give. Help
me to live with a clear sense of the hope that I have in
you. I need not fear hardship, the loss of possessions,
sickness, or even death itself. You have defeated death,
sin, and every evil power, and my future with you – even
beyond the grave – is certain. I rejoice because I know
that my labour in your name is not in vain. It will have
eternal consequences. Lord, let the hope that is within me
shape my life and my actions. Let me stand firm, like the
Chinese students and faculty noted above, and let
nothing move me from obedience to you. Enable me to
give myself, and all that I do, fully to you.

Meditation #29:
We Will Not Turn Back

On one occasion, while he was eating with them, he gave them this command: 'Do not leave Jerusalem, but wait for the gift my Father promised, which you have heard me speak about. For John baptised with water, but in a few days you will be baptised with the Holy Spirit.'

So when they met together, they asked him, 'Lord, are you at this time going to restore the kingdom to Israel?'

He said to them: 'It is not for you to know the times or dates the Father has set by his own authority. But you will receive power when the Holy Spirit comes on you; and you will be my witnesses in Jerusalem, and in all Judea and Samaria, and to the ends of the earth' (Acts 1:4–8).

The Wind of the Holy Spirit Will Blow Everywhere

From the East coast to the West coast
  The wind of the Holy Spirit will blow everywhere
From the East to the West
  The glory of the Holy Spirit will be released
Good news comes from heaven
  Good news rings in the ear
Causing dry bones to become moist
  Frail bones to become strong
Full of the Holy Spirit, we will not turn back

Step by step we go to distant places
The lame skipping
 The mute singing
The fire of the Holy Spirit, the longer it burns the brighter it
 gets.[1]

The Urging of the Holy Spirit

The Holy Spirit is urging
 Distant lands call
Asking for the sound of salvation to ring in their ears
 Countless pairs of expectant eyes
Oh, have not seen, have not heard the servants of God
 No matter what you feel
No matter what you see
 We must declare the good news everywhere
The Lord has already enabled us to see the land
 Oh, servants of God, you must boost your courage
The Lord has already won the victory
 Satan has been bound
Only one step further
 And we enter Canaan land.[2]

Lord, I thank you for pouring out your Spirit upon me. I am filled with joy because the Spirit lets me know that I am your child, loved by you. But Lord, help me remember that you have lavished your Spirit upon me not simply so that I may enjoy your presence. I know that you desire to lead and use me. You delight to grant me power through your Spirit so that I might be your witness. Lord, whether it be in distant lands or next door,

---

[1] Lu Xiaomin, *Sounds of the Heart*, 806 (Song #747).
[2] Lu Xiaomin, *Sounds of the Heart*, 826 (Song #767).

let my heart resonate with those of my Chinese brothers and sisters. Let my heart cry out along with theirs: I must declare the good news. Lord, anoint me. With your help I will not turn back.

Meditation #30:
Praise to the Lamb

After this I looked and there before me was a great multitude that no one could count, from every nation, tribe, people and language, standing before the throne and in front of the Lamb. They were wearing white robes and were holding palm branches in their hands. And they cried out in a loud voice:

'Salvation belongs to our God,
who sits on the throne,
and to the Lamb.'

All the angels were standing around the throne and around the elders and the four living creatures. They fell down on their faces before the throne and worshipped God, saying:

'Amen!
Praise and glory
and wisdom and thanks and honour
and power and strength
be to our God for ever and ever.
Amen!'
(Rev. 7:9–12).

One minority brother shared with me a powerful testimony of healing. When he was two years old he became very sick. His father took him to a hospital in the closest city. After the doctor examined the little boy, he told the father not to pay him, for his son would die. The doctor said he was virtually certain that the little boy would not survive. The sad father began the journey back home, carrying his sick little son. On the way the father noticed that the little boy had stopped breathing. He cried out to God and asked him to heal his son. He declared that if God would heal his son and allow him to live, he would dedicate the boy to God's service. When he arrived home and laid his son down, the little boy immediately asked for food. He quickly recovered and the father then gave him the name, Song Gao. He also retained the family name, according to Chinese custom; but the father gave him the name *Song* (praise) *Gao* (Lamb) or 'praise to the Lamb'. This little boy grew to adulthood and is now a powerful church leader.

Lord, I look forward to that day when I will join my Miao, Lisu, Mosuo and Tibetan brothers and sisters – and countless others from every nation, tribe, people and language group – and together with one voice we will sing of your greatness. I worship you for you are strong and powerful, like a roaring lion. But you are also loving and full of grace, like a lamb. The Lion of Judah and the Lamb that was slain, you perfectly embody true power and love. Salvation comes from you and you alone. For you and you alone are worthy. You alone purchased the nations with your blood. You alone hold the destiny of nations in your hand. Praise be to the Lamb.

Meditation #31:
A Lisu Farewell

Peter said to him, 'We have left everything to follow you!'
'I tell you the truth,' Jesus replied, 'no-one who has left home or brothers or sisters or mother or father or children or fields for me and the gospel will fail to receive a hundred times as much in this present age (homes, brothers, sisters, mothers, children and fields – and with them, persecutions) and in the age to come, eternal life. But many who are first will be last, and the last first' (Mk. 10:28–31).

Over the past four years on a regular basis I have travelled to a remote area inhabited by the Lisu people. A Bible training centre and a large group of churches dot the landscape of this mountainous region. I have had many opportunities to hike with fine Lisu pastors to distant villages in order to preach, sing and share fellowship with the believers living there. A number of these pastors have become very good friends. I am constantly amazed at their physical stamina. Pastor Ding, for example, is 70 years old, but he can still hike for six hours in one day at a pace that pushes me to my limit. I am also very much encouraged by their commitment to Christ, their willingness to sacrifice for the sake of the gospel, and their Christian love.

Just before I was scheduled to return to the US for a leave of absence, I travelled back to Lisu land to visit a group of churches. One stage of my journey involved hiking up a steep mountain path to a distant village. As usual, Pastor Mi was one of those who travelled with me. I always look forward to these hikes, not because I am particularly fond of physical pain, but because I enjoy being with men like Pastor Mi. And on journeys like these, God always seems to bring unexpected surprises our way.

This trip was no exception. After a service in one village, we travelled back down the mountain in a small jeep with six other people and a goat (quite a ride!). On the road we were greeted by a very excited man. He was a member of the Jingpo tribe and, having heard that we were coming, he came out to ask us to pray with his family. They were building a new home – it took one day to build their bamboo, thatch home – and wanted us to bless it. It was touching to see their eagerness and joy as we prayed. I sensed that to these people we represented Christ in a very unique way.

Later that night I preached at an evening service in another Lisu village. After the service I shared a meal with the leaders of the church. The building we ate in was a simple, mud brick dwelling with a tile roof. Holes in the wall served as a door and windows. A single, bare light bulb hung from the ceiling. In the darkness, the light shone brightly and attracted a battalion of insects. These bugs were both long and large, sporting a two inch wing-span. Thy swarmed overhead as we ate and talked. Occasionally, one would dip down low into our faces. My Lisu friends were hardly distracted. Then I saw one bug fly into the soup bowl in front of me. A man sitting to my left, using his chopsticks, deftly plucked the insect out of the soup, raised it up so he could examine it in the light, and then, after observing it for a few seconds, plopped it into his mouth and gobbled it up. No one batted an eye at this unusual feast.

The next day I prepared to leave my Lisu friends and travel back to my home. The journey to the closest airport was about two hours by car. Pastor Mi rode with me in the back seat. As the car bounced along the rough road, Mi looked over and said to me, 'You love us!'

Four years of sharing meals, hiking and ministering together, were all summed up in that short phrase. I responded, 'And you love us ... the love of Jesus is wonderful.'

Lord, I will gladly serve you. You delight to shower me with your blessings. All of your promises are true. To those whom you call to leave family, friends and fields, you truly do provide a hundred-fold return. You usher me into your presence as a member of your great family, you fill my life with close and joyful relationships, and you provide for my needs. Although you have promised persecution, this is for but a short time. Eternal life is my ultimate reward. Praise the name of the Lord.

Meditation #32:
Inside the 'Three Self' Church

For this reason, since the day we heard about you, we have not stopped praying for you and asking God to fill you with the knowledge of his will through all spiritual wisdom and understanding. And we pray this in order that you may live a life worthy of the Lord and may please him in every way: bearing fruit in every good work, growing in the knowledge of God, being strengthened with all power according to his glorious might so that you may have great endurance and patience, and joyfully giving thanks to the Father, who has qualified you to share in the inheritance of the saints in the kingdom of light. For he has rescued us from the dominion of darkness and brought us into the kingdom of the Son he loves, in whom we have redemption, the forgiveness of sins (Col. 1:9–14).

On one occasion I was invited by some TSPM church leaders from a rural county to speak to a gathering of women. Over 50 women from churches in remote villages in the county gathered together for a week of fellowship, Bible study and prayer. I gladly accepted the invitation, but knowing that this was a TSPM setting, wondered what I would find.

I arrived at the host church around 10:00 am and was greeted by several pastors and the local Religious Affairs Bureau (RAB) representative. The RAB representative was not a believer. His job was to represent the interests

of the Chinese government and ensure that nothing
'subversive' would take place. It was an unusual mix of
people – pastors, a missionary and a government official.
We sat around a table, ate sunflower seeds, drank tea and
tried to figure one another out as we engaged in stilted,
but friendly conversation. Later I learnt that the father of
one of the pastors present, a prominent church leader in
that area in the 1960s, had been executed by the 'Red
Guards' during the Cultural Revolution because he
would not renounce Jesus.

After more than an hour of discussion, we all walked
to the large classroom where the training sessions were
being held. It was an incredible scene. Over 50 women,
obviously key leaders in their respective churches, were
seated behind rows of desks. At the front of the room,
next to the blackboard, stood a middle-aged man. In
monosyllabic tones he read his notes for the day – a
government document filled with platitudes about
economic development. Fortunately for me and the
ladies, the man was bringing his presentation to a close. I
looked around and noticed that most of the women were
fighting sleep and boredom. The reader himself appeared
as uninterested in the proceedings as the women. I began
to wonder if my decision to come had been a mistake.

Mercifully the meeting came to an end. We all filed
down a flight of stairs and into another room for lunch.
After lunch I was told that I would be given the afternoon
teaching slot. The meeting began with songs of praise.
The atmosphere in the classroom changed dramatically
as the women began to sing of God and their faith. As I
moved forward to the front of the classroom I was filled
with a sense of kinship, a sense of communion with these
dear ladies. What a joy it was to be able to share from the
word of God to this remarkable group of Christian
women! I spoke from John's Gospel, a simple message

about faith and discipleship. The contrast with what had preceded was striking. As I spoke, I noticed that the RAB man was sitting in the back, listening to every word. At one stage I was quite animated, and in the middle of my point the RAB man stood up and walked out of the room. I must confess that my first thought was, 'Oh no, I'm in big trouble now.' But later he returned and remained very cordial. A few days later the local pastor called and expressed his appreciation for my willingness to share with the ladies.

Shortly after this experience I travelled to a remote village for a Sunday morning church service. The village was not very large and I anticipated a small group that morning, perhaps 40 or 50 at most. When I entered the church building I was startled to see that it was absolutely packed. From the outside the building had looked rather small, but once inside, I found that the sanctuary was quite long and that it contained a balcony. Altogether there were well over 200 believers present. I was amazed because this was clearly more than the population of the village. Later I learnt that this church was the centre of Christian life in the area and that many believers from nearby villages also worshipped there. I was asked to preach and spoke from Revelation 5 about the power and love of Christ.

After the service I shared a meal with a group of elders from the various village churches represented. They indicated that their greatest need was for biblical teaching. I told them about my experience at the women's conference and asked them if they could hold a similar training session in their church. After all, they were also a recognized TSPM church. They indicated that they were unwilling to ask the TSPM leadership for help with training because they said 'the TSPM teaches things that are contrary to the Bible'. I knew they were referring to the kind of thing I had recently witnessed: a government official offering, at best, irrelevant platitudes from Beijing to the saints.

Lord, when I think of the TSPM churches in China, I rejoice because I know that you are working in and through the lives of many believers there. I ask that you guide them and grant them courage, for they walk a difficult path. Help them take advantage of the many opportunities they have to openly worship your name. Grant them wisdom so that they may distinguish between essential matters and those that are relatively unimportant. Strengthen those who face difficulties because they are unwilling to conform to government restrictions. Enable them to be fruitful and fill them with your joy. And Lord, I ask that you would strengthen me. Help me bear fruit and joyfully give thanks to you.

Meditation #33:
Light in a Dark, Smoky Room

'When he came to his senses, he said, "How many of my father's hired men have food to spare, and here I am starving to death! I will set out and go back to my father and say to him: Father, I have sinned against heaven and against you. I am no longer worthy to be called your son; make me like one of your hired men." So he got up and went to his father.

'But while he was still a long way off, his father saw him and was filled with compassion for him; he ran to his son, threw his arms around him and kissed him.

'The son said to him, "Father, I have sinned against heaven and against you. I am no longer worthy to be called your son."

'But the father said to his servants, "Quick! Bring the best robe and put it on him. Put a ring on his finger and sandals on his feet. Bring the fattened calf and kill it. Let's have a feast and celebrate. For this son of mine was dead and is alive again; he was lost and is found." So they began to celebrate' (Lk. 15:17–24).

Earlier last year I, along with another brother, travelled to a minority village in a remote part of China. The village was very small, consisting of ten homes and around 40 people. I stayed with the Luo family, clearly the leaders of the village. The village was very poor, without electricity. The villagers were subsistence farmers. They had almost no knowledge of Christianity.

The first night we shared a video (using a battery pack and projector) about creation, the fall, the life of Jesus and a final summary of the gospel. The reaction was mixed. Later, however, we sat around the fire in the Luo family home and talked. The villagers began to open up and share more about their lives and their struggles. We finally had a time of prayer.

The next day was tremendous. A pig was slaughtered (an annual event) and packed for preservation and usage throughout the year. Then we all came together for a great feast. That night about 25 villagers gathered in the dimly lit main room of our host's home. Oil lamps and an open fire filled the room with smoke, but also provided our only light. My colleague, Laurence, had his guitar so we began to sing. These are oral people, used to sitting around the fire at night and singing and talking. And so, after a song or two, I began to tell them stories about Jesus. This took the entire evening. Laurence was the singer, I was the story-teller. The villagers loved the songs and the parables of Jesus. It was wonderful to see their interest and amazement as they heard, for the very first time, the parables of the prodigal son, the unmerciful servant, and the great banquet. I ended by emphasizing that God does not look down upon people. He loves all those he created, including their tribe. By following Jesus we can have our relationship with God restored and become a part of his family. We ended with a time of prayer. There was a wonderful sense of God's presence in that dark, smoky room packed with villagers.

Lord, I praise you because you love all of your creation, including those in the poorest villages of this world. You are not impressed by demonstrations of power and wealth, nor are you blinded by outward displays of piety. You look upon the heart. And you welcome the poor and the rich alike, to lay aside other priorities and joyfully enter into your family. Lord, help me celebrate with you when lost siblings return to the family. Enable me to see others as you see them, and thus seek for their return – and celebrate to the extreme when they do so.

Meditation #34:
Pentecost in the Mountains

When the day of Pentecost came, they were all together in one place. Suddenly a sound like the blowing of a violent wind came from heaven and filled the whole house where they were sitting. They saw what seemed to be tongues of fire that separated and came to rest on each of them. All of them were filled with the Holy Spirit and began to speak in other tongues as the Spirit enabled them.

Now there were staying in Jerusalem God-fearing Jews from every nation under heaven. When they heard this sound, a crowd came together in bewilderment, because each one heard them speaking in his own language. Utterly amazed, they asked: 'Are not all these men who are speaking Galileans?' … Amazed and perplexed, they asked one another, 'What does this mean?'

Some, however, made fun of them and said, 'They have had too much wine' (Acts 2:1–8, 12–13).

On one occasion I arranged for a team to minister in a Miao village that I had visited in the past. The team was made up of 12 people. Because of our numbers, I arranged for a van to take us as far up the mountain as possible. The village we were to visit was located high in the mountains in a remote and very poor area of our province. The road conditions were rough and finally, with a gasp, the driver pulled over and said that he had driven as far as possible. We would need to hike the rest of the way.

After a short hike, we arrived to the sort of welcome that only the Miao can give. Believers lined the path singing songs of welcome and encouragement. They led us in this manner into the church. Although the population of the village is less than 200, a sea of over 250 smiling faces had packed into the church. This village and its church are at the centre of Christian activity in the area and many come from surrounding villages to worship there.

The service began and I was quickly reminded that there are few things so humbling as participating in a Miao worship service. You see, the Miao assume that everyone can sing. They are wonderful singers and their choirs are renowned for the exquisite beauty of their songs. It does no good to protest – visitors must always contribute at least one song. I had prepared the group in advance, so we marched up to the front of the church and sang our Chinese renditions of a few simple choruses. Afterwards, the Miao choir assembled at the front and began to sing. The power and beauty of their worship was breathtaking. Our team sat in awe as these simple people from the mountains – a people who, prior to receiving the gospel a little over one hundred years ago, were viewed as savages – sang songs that would have been welcomed in any cathedral in the world. And then their children's choir sang. It was wonderful.

When the singing came to an end our team began to share about God's love and his power to change lives. After a couple of testimonies, my friend spoke from Acts 2 on Pentecost. He shared how God had been pouring out his Spirit on many – men, women and children – in their church and encouraged the Miao believers to open their hearts to God's gifts. In spite of the simplicity of my translation, the message struck a chord in the hearts of the Miao. After the message, we asked for those who wanted prayer to stand. The entire congregation rose to their feet. Our team fanned out among the people and we all began to lay hands on the people and pray. The Spirit filled the place and many began to cry, shake and worship with a loud voice. It was Pentecost all over again, but this time in the mountains of China. I had never seen anything like this in a Miao church. The Miao tend to be rather formal and reserved in manner and worship. But here, an incredible sense of hunger for and openness to the things of the Spirit permeated the place. Formalities were laid aside as people entered into the presence of God.

In the midst of all this I noticed the driver of our van standing in the congregation and, with wide eyes, was taking it all in. I walked over and asked him what he thought about all that was going on. He replied, 'This is wonderful. I am deeply moved.' I asked him if he knew Jesus. He replied, 'No, not yet; but I am ready!' The impact on him of God's presence and the authentic worship was evident. I shared the gospel with this man and then led him in the sinner's prayer. His face radiated with joy as we returned home that day.

Lord, send your Spirit again as on the day of Pentecost. I offer my life to you. Anoint me and use me for your purposes. Reveal your power through signs and wonders. Lead me with visions and dreams. And, above all, let me serve as your herald, your prophet, declaring your mighty deeds. Lord, I acknowledge that I am weak, but I recognize your strength. As your servant, filled with your Spirit, I know that I can fulfil the tasks you have for me. So, fill me now. Pour out your Spirit once again.

Meditation #35:
'Tis the Season

Who has believed our message
   and to whom has the arm of the LORD been revealed?
He grew up before him like a tender shoot,
   and like a root out of dry ground.
He had no beauty or majesty to attract us to him,
   nothing in his appearance that we should desire him.
He was despised and rejected by men,
   a man of sorrows, and familiar with suffering.
Like one from whom men hide their faces
   he was despised, and we esteemed him not.
Surely he took up our infirmities
   and carried our sorrows,
yet we considered him stricken by God,
   smitten by him, and afflicted.
But he was pierced for our transgressions,
   he was crushed for our iniquities;
the punishment that brought us peace was upon him,
   and by his wounds we are healed.
We all, like sheep, have gone astray,
   each of us has turned to his own way;
and the LORD has laid on him
   the iniquity of us all (Is. 53:1–6)

In one region of China, the Christmas season marks a major transition for a number of dedicated young Chinese Christians: it is the time when they lay aside their hoes, say 'goodbye' to family, and travel from their home villages to rural Bible schools. Recently, I received a letter from a Chinese pastor that offers a glimpse at life in these schools. As I read the letter, I was challenged by the simplicity of the students' lives, and by the willingness of their teachers to sacrifice comfort and security for the sake of the gospel. These Chinese Christians, who have so little in terms of material possessions and yet who are so rich in terms of faith and Christian community, call us to remember the manner in which Jesus entered into the world – as a child in a lowly manger – and the lifestyle he modelled. This message is especially relevant in our affluent western culture, where Christmas is so often associated with consumerism and materialism. I have translated the following excerpts from my friend's letter:

In [our area] there are two 'short-term' Bible schools: L Bible School and Y Bible School. The L school has a total of 114 students and serves the Jingpo and Lisu minority groups, as well as the Han Chinese. The training programme runs for three months and the total cost (including living expenses) per student for this three-month period is US $25. The students live very simply. Their meals normally consist of vegetables (only one dish per meal). Meat is a luxury which they eat only once a week. The school has two teachers, who live on less than US $12 per month.

The conditions at Y Bible School are slightly better. However, the teachers there are not paid any salary and only receive the food they need in order to survive. In spite of these difficult circumstances, the morale of the teachers has remained high. The school has 100 students, including both Jingpo and Lisu Christians.

The students study at these schools three months each year (from January through March) for a period of three years. Thus, the students complete the nine-month programme over the course of three years. The L school has been training Christian leaders for six years, the Y school for a period of three years. The results have been tremendous.

Lord, I worship you for you did not enter our world with a dazzling display of your power. You did not come with brute force as a conqueror; you came in weakness and you were willing to suffer on my behalf. You were despised and rejected. I too sinned against you. And yet you bore my sins and received the punishment that was justly mine. And through this, you brought me peace – peace with you and peace with my neighbours. Lord, help me live a life of service for you. Enable me too to reach out with grace to those who despise me. Give me strength so that I too might be willing to become weak before others, and even suffer if need be, for you and the sake of the gospel.

Meditation #36:
One Small Step

What shall we say, then? Shall we go on sinning so that grace may increase? By no means! We died to sin; how can we live in it any longer? Or don't you know that all of us who were baptised into Christ Jesus were baptised into his death? We were therefore buried with him through baptism into death in order that, just as Christ was raised from the dead through the glory of the Father, we too may live a new life.

If we have been united with him like this in his death, we will certainly also be united with him in his resurrection. For we know that our old self was crucified with him so that the body of sin might be done away with, that we should no longer be slaves to sin – because anyone who has died has been freed from sin.

Now if we died with Christ, we believe that we will also live with him (Rom. 6:1–8).

The group of 75 Chinese believers gathered by the cool waters. Earlier that morning the venue for this service had been hastily changed. They had been warned by friends that the place where they had originally planned to meet was not safe. And so, new arrangements had been made. Now, all thoughts of security and logistics were left aside. Certainly there was no fear, only thanksgiving and joy.

One by one the 12 new converts shared testimonies of God's grace. Then a tall, slender young lady stepped before the crowd. She was not Chinese, but she was part of the family. She too shared of God's love and her desire to please him. She was 15 and ready to make a public stand for Christ. Her blonde-headed, 13-year-old sister followed in her footsteps. There was much laughter and rejoicing. It was a time for celebration, a time for thanksgiving. The believers listened attentively as the little blonde girl told of her love for Jesus and her desire to serve him in all things.

Then, all of them, 14 in all, each in turn, took the biggest step of their lives and entered into the water. Baptism in China has special significance, for it is viewed as the definitive declaration of one's faith. In a country where people are persecuted for being Christians – sometimes by family members, sometimes by government officials – it is a moment marked with meaning. It signifies one's willingness to identify with Christ, even in the face of suffering and death. And as Paul reminds us, it also bears witness to the new life, eternal life, which only God can give: 'We were therefore buried with him through baptism into death in order that, just as Christ was raised from the dead through the glory of the Father, we too may live a new life' (Rom. 6:4).

It was just one small step into the water, but a step with eternal significance. My daughters chose to take that step in China.

Lord, I thank you for enabling me to identify with your death and resurrection in the rite of water baptism. Help me remember that it is because you died for me that I now live. Let me be mindful that it is because you rose from the dead that I now live a new life, free from the bondage of sin. Lord, I rejoice that I am able to publicly declare my faith in you – definitively in water baptism, but also daily through a transformed life. Thank you for enabling me to take this step. Help me to continue to walk in the Spirit.

Meditation #37:
A Fruitful Life

We always thank God, the Father of our Lord Jesus Christ, when we pray for you, because we have heard of your faith in Christ Jesus and of the love you have for all the saints – the faith and love that spring from the hope that is stored up for you in heaven and that you have already heard about in the word of truth, the gospel that has come to you. All over the world this gospel is bearing fruit and growing, just as it has been doing among you since the day you heard it and understood God's grace in all its truth (Col. 1:3–6).

A number of years ago I was privileged to travel to a particularly remote rural county, home to over 18 minority groups, in order to explore possibilities for future ministry. The county's name literally means 'War' and 'Peace'. The name reflects the region's history. The minority groups which populate the region (the Yi and Miao being the most prominent) were integrated into the Chinese empire through military suppression and then entered into a period of relative peace. Although war is no longer a present concern, life in this area is hard. The annual per capita income at the time of my visit was less than US $40. A quarter of the population lives without electricity, educational opportunities are limited and the villagers struggle simply to survive. Spiritually, the darkness of spiritism and the void left by Marxist atheism are both evident. Nevertheless, in the midst of enormous physical and spiritual needs, I saw indications that the gospel is changing lives and bringing hope.

In virtually every village I visited, signs of the vitality of the church and spiritual life could be seen. This was the case in spite of the ever watchful and obtrusive government officials who attempted to direct my every move. One Yi cluster of mud huts was home to 220 villagers. Of this group, 80 were Christians. While I was walking through the village, an elderly lady invited me into her home, a mud hovel, for some tea. Since I was at the rear of our group and the government officials were far ahead, I sensed this would be a good opportunity for uncensored conversation. I called to a Christian friend, and together we entered the lady's hut. In the dark and dingy dwelling we talked as her husband heated up some water for tea. Other members of the extended family soon appeared. I noted in Mandarin that my friend and I were Americans. They looked puzzled. One lady indicated that she had never heard of America! When I spoke to my friend in English, the family thought I was speaking another dialect of Yi and were surprised that they could not understand. They seemed to think we were from another Yi tribe or village. Finally, we were able to communicate to them that we were 'foreigners'. They then asked if we were the ones they had seen on TV (in most of the villages, however poor, at least one hut shelters a television set). We assured them that we were not, but they were still surprised when we refused their offer of cigarettes, as the TV commercials they had seen suggested that all foreigners smoked. Knowing that the officials might come at any moment, we quickly inquired concerning their faith and Christianity in the village. It was exciting to find that here were people who had never heard of America and yet the gospel was not unknown to them.

The next day we hiked up to a Miao village. As we climbed up the steep mountain trail, we noticed a white building in the centre of a village on an adjacent mountain. It was a church. We learnt that in 1902 a British missionary had brought the gospel to the Miao living on the mountain. Later we would learn that there were many Christians in the area, including the village we visited, and that every Sunday they travelled to this church for services. On the way down the mountain I gazed at the white church and considered the lasting effect of the missionary's work. He probably never saw the real fruit of his labours. Yet in the face of every form of opposition, the gospel he proclaimed has taken root – and it continues to bear fruit. I thanked the Lord for bringing my family to China and prayed that he would enable us to have a similar impact.

Lord, I thank you for the power of the gospel to bring hope and change lives. I am thankful that someone shared this message with me and that it is now bearing fruit in my life. And I rejoice because your gospel is bearing fruit and growing around the world. Even in the most remote and poverty-stricken areas, your gospel is at work bringing hope and life. Lord, I thank you for the life of the British missionary who brought the gospel to the remote, Miao village noted above. I pray that my life might also be fruitful for you.

Meditation #38:
Travelling the Way of the Masses

Though I am free and belong to no man, I make myself a slave to everyone, to win as many as possible. To the Jews I became like a Jew, to win the Jews. To those under the law I became like one under the law (though I myself am not under the law), so as to win those under the law. To those not having the law I became like one not having the law (though I am not free from God's law but am under Christ's law), so as to win those not having the law. To the weak I became weak, to win the weak. I have become all things to all men so that by all possible means I might save some. I do all this for the sake of the gospel, that I may share in its blessings (1 Cor. 9:19–23).

Travelling in China is always interesting. This is especially the case when you travel the way of the masses. A while back I travelled from the western part of China to Shanghai (virtually the whole width of China) by bus, train (hard berth) and boat. The boat trip was unique. My fourth-class ticket provided me with a small bunk in the midst of a mass of humanity. Privacy was non-existent. The only opportunity to change my clothes came under the cover of my blanket. I frequently heard the Chinese around me complain, 'ren tai dou le' (too many people)! Once in the washroom, I understood why. Even at six in the morning it was difficult to find a spot near a sink to shave. The room was packed with people standing three or four deep before the sinks, waiting for an opening to appear. After a considerable time, I inched my way into a tiny space which had just opened up in front of a sink. The crowd continued to press in. I constantly had to keep alert so as not to lose my position. On more than one occasion I would have been knocked down had the wall of people not held me up.

On land, I fared much better. My accommodations were very basic but relatively clean and, by comparison to the boat, spacious. I certainly couldn't complain about the price. When was the last time you spent a night in a guesthouse or hotel for US $1.50? And at that price they even left the light on.

Lord, there are so many things that serve to isolate me from others, especially those living in darkness. My affluence separates me from the poor. My religiosity separates me from sinners. My business separates me from my neighbour. Lord, help me break through the barriers that keep me apart. Let me be sensitive to your leading. Direct me to those who are in need. Enable me to travel the way of the masses so that I might bless others in your name.

Meditation #39:
Persecuted, Yet Persevering

Therefore, brothers, since we have confidence to enter the Most Holy Place by the blood of Jesus, by a new and living way opened for us through the curtain, that is, his body, and since we have a great priest over the house of God, let us draw near to God with a sincere heart in full assurance of faith, having our hearts sprinkled to cleanse us from a guilty conscience and having our bodies washed with pure water. Let us hold unswervingly to the hope we profess, for he who promised is faithful. And let us consider how we may spur one another on towards love and good deeds. Let us not give up meeting together, as some are in the habit of doing, but let us encourage one another – and all the more as you see the Day approaching (Heb. 10:19–25).

Not along ago I spoke with Brother Tao, one of the original seven members of the Wenzhou Church. The Wenzhou Church is one of the many vibrant and rapidly growing house church groups in China. Brother Tao spoke of the church's origin and history. He indicated that there had been some strong evangelical influence in Wenzhou prior to the communist era. However, their church really started around 1970, when in the context of the Cultural Revolution and great persecution, a group of seven began to meet together in a home. Brother Tao noted that they were largely untaught, but depended on the Holy Spirit. He indicated that they emphasized repentance, faith in Christ and being born again, as well as the power of the Holy Spirit, baptism in the Spirit, speaking in tongues and spiritual gifts. I asked Brother Tao how they came to these theological beliefs. He answered, 'From a simple reading of the Bible.' He said that they (the original seven) chose to follow what they felt was clearly taught in Scripture.

Brother Tao stated that after 1976 the Three Self church began to operate more openly in their area. Some of their people joined the TSPM church, but most continued to meet in homes. As a result of their unwillingness to join the TSPM and conform to government regulations, they continue to face intense persecution. Yet Brother Tao obviously feels that they made the right choice. He suggested that they (that is, the house church believers) were the true 'Three Self' or 'indigenous' church.

The Wenzhou Church has experienced rapid growth, although it is not a tightly connected group like some of the other house church networks. For example, they do not appear to have Wenzhou churches in other areas, but rather they assist and encourage churches to develop an autonomous identity in their own region. Clearly, they have also experienced a lot of persecution. Brother Tao, in particular, has been in prison on several occasions and is a 'marked' man. And yet here he was, in a distant area of China, proclaiming the gospel and encouraging the saints.

Lord, I am so thankful that because of your death on my behalf, I can enter into your presence. You have cleansed me, so now I can draw near to you. Forgive me for standing aloof too often. Forgive me for not hungering more for your presence. As I read Brother Tao's story, I am reminded how lightly I take my freedom to worship together with other believers. Lord, help me cherish the opportunities I have to worship you and fellowship with others. Help me draw close to you.

Meditation #40:
The Power of the Holy Spirit

On their release, Peter and John went back to their own people and reported all that the chief priests and elders had said to them. When they heard this, they raised their voices together in prayer to God. 'Sovereign Lord,' they said, 'you made the heaven and the earth and the sea, and everything in them. ... Now, Lord, consider their threats and enable your servants to speak your word with great boldness. Stretch out your hand to heal and perform miraculous signs and wonders through the name of your holy servant Jesus.'

After they prayed, the place where they were meeting was shaken. And they were all filled with the Holy Spirit and spoke the word of God boldly (Acts 4:23–24, 29–31).

The Power of the Holy Spirit

Power, power, the Holy Spirit's power
   Full of support and comfort
Leading you and leading me
   The world cannot see clearly
The world cannot comprehend
   This is a kind of immeasurable power
Power, power, it comes from Jehovah
   Power, power, on Jehovah's troops

He clothes his sons and daughters with this power
  In this time of darkness, rays of light shine into the distance
The Holy Spirit's power, great and incomparable
  Holds together all things, created the heavens and the earth
The hearts of men are laid bare before Him
  No one is able to run and hide
The Holy Spirit's power renews you and me
  The Holy Spirit's power shakes you and me
He has directed us to walk on the right path
  He leads us directly towards the new heaven and new earth.[1]

We Will Evangelize the Nations

Spreading the gospel is our battle cry
  We will evangelize all the nations of the world
We will leap over high mountains
  Go to every place on the planet
Until everyone under heaven knows
  We of China will evangelize the nations
We of this generation will evangelize the nations
  The fire in his hand is already kindled
We will evangelize the nations.[2]

Lord, I acknowledge that I am weak. Oh, but you are strong. I desperately need your strength. Oh, but you delight to provide the strength I need. So I rejoice, for you have promised to grant power through your Spirit in my time of need. Lord, I call upon you. The challenges before

---

[1] Lu Xiaomin, *Sounds of the Heart*, 21 (Song #16).
[2] Lu Xiaomin, *Sounds of the Heart*, 213 (Song #187).

me are too great; the task is too large. Anoint me and lead me. Give me the boldness of my Chinese brothers and sisters. Shake my world so that I might be used for your glory.

Meditation #41:
Advancing the Gospel

Now I want you to know, brothers, that what has happened to me has really served to advance the gospel. As a result, it has become clear throughout the whole palace guard and to everyone else that I am in chains for Christ. Because of my chains, most of the brothers in the Lord have been encouraged to speak the word of God more courageously and fearlessly.

It is true that some preach Christ out of envy and rivalry, but others out of goodwill. The latter do so in love, knowing that I am put here for the defence of the gospel. The former preach Christ out of selfish ambition, not sincerely, supposing that they can stir up trouble for me while I am in chains. But what does it matter? The important thing is that in every way, whether from false motives or true, Christ is preached. And because of this I rejoice (Phil. 1:12–18).

During a visit to a church in a small town in China, I met a Christian brother who was clearly a very active and respected church leader in that area. He was about 40 years of age. I wanted to speak to this man privately, but it seemed that we were always surrounded by government officials and other church leaders. On one occasion, however, on leaving the church to go to another building, we found ourselves alone. As we walked, he told me a remarkable story.

The former pastor of the church in that area was arrested by the Red Guards during the Cultural Revolution decade (1966–76). They tried to persuade him to renounce his faith. Even though the pastor was beaten and threatened, he refused to renounce Christ. Finally, the Red Guards paraded him through the streets of the small town and denounced him. Then, before the eyes of all (including his teenage son), this Chinese pastor was publicly executed.

His teenage son was the man now telling me the story. As he described the scene and the cries of the believers as they witnessed the execution, tears streamed down his face. The recounting of this story had rekindled deep emotions. While we continued to talk, I thought of this man's situation. It was entirely possible that some of the men he routinely met on the street were formerly Red Guards who had helped execute his father. So I wondered, was he bitter? Was he angry? I searched for signs of bitterness. Yet I left sensing that the answer to these questions was 'no'. This man has now taken his father's place. He is the key leader in an area where Christianity is now exploding. As he shared his story there was no evidence of anger, he simply stressed the effect of his father's death on the church: tremendous growth!

Lord, grant me the grace to love my enemies. Help me not to lash out at those who persecute me. Let me be mindful that it is through circumstances like these that the gospel is advanced. Lord, I thank you for the witness of this Chinese pastor and his son. In their lives and their responses to persecution, I see your love and grace.

Meditation #42:
Hard Pressed

We do not want you to be uninformed, brothers, about the hardships we suffered in the province of Asia. We were under great pressure, far beyond our ability to endure, so that we despaired even of life. Indeed, in our hearts we felt the sentence of death. But this happened that we might not rely on ourselves but on God, who raises the dead. He has delivered us from such a deadly peril, and he will deliver us. On him we have set our hope that he will continue to deliver us, as you help us by your prayers. Then many will give thanks on our behalf for the gracious favour granted us in answer to the prayers of many (2 Cor. 1:8–11).

Not long ago house church leaders from two different networks met together in my home. It was fascinating watching how they interacted with one another. Three key questions were commonly asked. It was apparent that these three questions touched upon matters they viewed as significant and foundational for church leadership. First, they asked about their conversion experience. Second, they wanted to know about their call to ministry. Finally, they asked about their experience of persecution (that is, their time in prison). Their conversion, their call and their suffering – these were the marks of a true minister. I could not help but compare this list with the list of qualifications we generally look for in church leaders in the West. There was something very basic, very compelling and very New Testament about their approach.

About six months ago, Mr He, a high-level leader of one of the largest house church networks in China visited my apartment. The senior leader in their fellowship had recently been imprisoned. His imprisonment signalled a new wave of persecution directed at this particular group. Mr He, a stocky, middle-aged man, sat in my living room and shared how this new wave of persecution was affecting his life. He was now on the run and his future was very uncertain. He had spent time in prison in the past and he was prepared to return if need be. He told of how his apartment was watched and how he had been harassed. The last time he was arrested, a group of police officers burst into his apartment at 1:00 am in the morning. His 15-year-old daughter woke up and was terrified as she saw the officers dragging her father from their home. The pastor was deeply moved by this memory. The thoughts of his traumatized daughter and her perceptions as she watched him being dragged away as a criminal were still fresh in his mind. His comments jolted me, for I too have a 15-year-old. I cannot imagine what that experience must have been like.

More recently, a Bible school operated by one of the house church networks in our area was raided by the police. The 30 students and three faculty members of the school were all arrested. Most of the students were released after a week, but two students and two faculty members were kept in custody in very difficult conditions for over a month. One faculty member was kept under house arrest for three months. Some of the students and faculty were interrogated for up to 48 hours in one sitting and were not provided with adequate food or clothing. This sort of treatment is not unusual, but rather the norm.

Lord, I know that I do not understand what it means to suffer for the sake of the gospel like my Chinese friends do. And, perhaps as a result, I too often rely on myself and my own plans and strength. Lord, teach me to depend on you. Teach me to live with a sense of holy abandonment, completely dedicated to your calling. And teach me to pray. Oh, Lord, teach me to pray.

I ask for your blessing upon Mr He and his family. Strengthen them and deliver them from the perils they face.

Meditation #43:
Better and Lasting Possessions

Remember those earlier days after you had received the light, when you stood your ground in a great contest in the face of suffering. Sometimes you were publicly exposed to insult and persecution; at other times you stood side by side with those who were so treated. You sympathised with those in prison and joyfully accepted the confiscation of your property, because you knew that you yourselves had better and lasting possessions (Heb. 10:32–34).

At 2:00 am, early on the morning of the 13th, the work group [98 comrades] separated into three groups and boldly and powerfully launched their attack, rushing towards their prearranged objectives: the villages of Suo Ma, Yang Pu, and Tai An. Two believers in Suo Ma village, Li Hu Gan and Li Hu Liu, grabbed a knife and attempted to block the work group from carrying out their official business. These men were lawfully arrested.

This is how the *Hong He County Newspaper* (30 June 1998 issue, page 4) in an article entitled, 'Our County's Lawful Efforts to Punish Illegal Religious Activity in Luo En Township Meet with Initial Success', described the tragic events which took place in the early hours of 13 June 1998. Yet the plight of Li Hu Liu, one of the Christians attacked and arrested in this pre-dawn raid, casts further light on these deeply disturbing events in

Hong He County (Yunnan Province, China). Local believers provided the following chilling account of the last days in the life of Li Hu Liu, a 23-year-old Christian man.

Around 3:00 am on 13 June, Public Security Bureau (PSB) officers burst into the home of Li Hu Liu. Initially, he was startled and, not knowing who his attackers were, he grabbed a knife. After the officers burst in they quickly knocked him to the floor. Although by this time he had dropped his knife and was not resisting them, they continued to beat him, savagely kicking him in the groin.

Later that morning, a badly beaten Mr Li was placed in prison. In spite of his injuries, he was not offered any medical care. While in prison, Mr Li was repeatedly beaten by the officers. Shortly before his death, Mr Li told a visitor to pass on a message to his father. (The pre-dawn raid had actually been designed to trap his father, a prominent Christian leader in the area. However, Li's father was staying with friends at the time and was not captured.) Mr Li told the visitor to warn his father not to return home. If his father returned home, Li warned, the local authorities would surely arrest him and beat him to death.

On the evening of 30 September 1998, shortly after this visit, Mr Li died. When the PSB notified the family of Li's death, family members asked, 'How did he die?'

The PSB simply responded, 'He died of sickness.'

The family asked for a hospital record indicating the cause of death, but none was available. Although the family stated that they wanted to bury the body, the PSB disposed of the corpse at 10:00 pm on the night of Mr Li's death and did not allow the family to view the body.

Mr Li's father was forced into hiding. Such is life for one Christian family in Southwest China.

Lord, I lift up the Li family and the other believers in Hong He County to you. I ask that you would comfort them and strengthen them in the midst of their hardship. Fill their lives with the hope that only you can give. Replace their suffering with joy and build your church. And Lord, help me be willing to face public ridicule for your sake. Give me strength so that I am able to stand firm when persecution comes. And even now, grant me the courage to stand side by side with those who are mistreated because they bear your name. Help me to do so, even if it is costly, even if it means that I too must suffer loss. Lord, help my life be shaped by the knowledge that I have better and lasting possessions.

Meditation #44:
The Double Promise

He went to Nazareth, where he had been brought up, and on the Sabbath day he went into the synagogue, as was his custom. And he stood up to read. The scroll of the prophet Isaiah was handed to him. Unrolling it, he found the place where it is written:

'The Spirit of the Lord is on me,
  because he has anointed me
  to preach good news to the poor.
He has sent me to proclaim freedom for the prisoners
  and recovery of sight for the blind,
to release the oppressed,
  to proclaim the year of the Lord's favour.'

Then he rolled up the scroll, gave it back to the attendant and sat down. The eyes of everyone in the synagogue were fastened on him, and he began by saying to them, 'Today this scripture is fulfilled in your hearing.' … All the people in the synagogue were furious when they heard this. They got up, drove him out of the town, and took him to the brow of the hill on which the town was built, in order to throw him down the cliff. But he walked right through the crowd and went on his way (Lk. 4:16–21, 28–30).

On 26 November 2002, I met with the top leader of the China for Christ house church network, Brother Zhang.

We met and discussed various items for about an hour and a half and then shared a meal together. While we were eating, Sister Ding, the second highest leader in the China for Christ network, joined us.

During our meal Sister Ding, who was sitting next to me, indicated that their church was Pentecostal in nature. They emphasize that just as the disciples were empowered by the Spirit on the day of Pentecost (Acts 2:1–21), so also believers today may receive the Spirit's power. Sister D then stated emphatically that their church came to these Pentecostal convictions not on the basis of receiving this tradition from others, but rather as a result of their own experience and study of the book of Acts. She indicated that in the 1970s and 1980s they were quite isolated and experienced considerable persecution. In this context of persecution they developed their Pentecostal theology and their church began to grow. Today, the China for Christ network is widely recognized as the largest house church group in China.

I then asked them if they felt the majority of Christians in China were Pentecostal. Brother Zhang answered and said that apart from the TSPM churches and various smaller house church groups, the vast majority were indeed Pentecostal. He considered several of the other large house church networks – the China Gospel Fellowship, the Li Xin Church and the Yin Shang Church – to be Pentecostal as well.

On another occasion late in 2002, I had the joy of teaching in an underground Bible school associated with the China for Christ network. During one of the breaks, the leader of the school showed me round and introduced me to some of the other faculty members. I still remember how, with great excitement, he spoke of the hunger for the things of the Spirit in the churches in the countryside.

I am convinced that there is a correlation between the house church's experience of persecution and their emphasis and dependence on the power of the Spirit. I pray that the experience of the church in China will challenge and inspire Christians in the West to embrace the double promise of Pentecost: the anointing of the Spirit brings power and opposition. The Chinese church reminds us that it is difficult to maintain one without the other.

Lord, I acknowledge that I desperately need the power and direction of your Spirit in my life. Forgive me for too often thinking primarily of my own comfort, my own well-being, my own advancement. Pour out your Spirit upon me – the Spirit who desires to activate your redeeming love within me and move me to reach out to a lost and dying world. Let it rain, Lord, let it rain. Fill me with your Spirit. Grip my heart with the needs of others, at home and around the world. And use me, Lord, use me for your glory.

Meditation #45:
The Need to Celebrate

When one of those at the table with him heard this, he said to Jesus, 'Blessed is the man who will eat at the feast in the kingdom of God.'

Jesus replied: 'A certain man was preparing a great banquet and invited many guests. At the time of the banquet he sent his servant to tell those who had been invited, "Come, for everything is now ready."

'But they all alike began to make excuses. The first said, "I have just bought a field, and I must go and see it. Please excuse me."

'Another said, "I have just bought five yoke of oxen, and I'm on my way to try them out. Please excuse me."

'Still another said, "I just got married, so I can't come."

'The servant came back and reported this to his master. Then the owner of the house became angry and ordered his servant, "Go out quickly into the streets and alleys of the town and bring in the poor, the crippled, the blind and the lame."

'"Sir," the servant said, "what you ordered has been done, but there is still room."

'Then the master told his servant, "Go out to the roads and country lanes and make them come in, so that my house will be full. I tell you, not one of those men who were invited will get a taste of my banquet"' (Lk. 14:15–24).

We walked through the door of the small apartment and entered the main room. The apartment was very simple, with concrete floors and bare walls. The walls of the main room were now adorned with Christmas decorations. One banner proclaimed, '*Pu Tian Tong Qing*' (The whole world celebrates [his birth] together). As I sat down on a small stool and looked at the crowd of people packing into the small apartment, I contemplated the truth of the banner's message. All over the world in every conceivable kind of place – from majestic cathedrals to simple makeshift chapels like this – people are celebrating Jesus' birth. The crowd grew to such a size that the small adjoining rooms had to be pressed into service. All told, around 70 people packed into the little sanctuary.

This house church is situated on the edge of a large city. The people living in this area represent simple village folks who have migrated to the city. Urbanization is taking place at a breathtaking pace in China. In urban centres throughout the land there are large populations of village people attempting to 'make it' in the city. It was apparent that these folks were marked more by the village than the city.

The service began and a sense of joy quickly permeated the small makeshift sanctuary. Songs and Scripture readings celebrating Christ's birth followed. Then came my turn to preach. I greeted the crowd, which now seemed like a large family, and began to share about Christmas. I highlighted the fact that Christmas represents a very wonderful and precious invitation; God's invitation to become a part of his family. I concluded with the parable of the great banquet (Lk.14:15–24) which emphasizes that we must respond to this invitation with joy, for there is no other appropriate response.

After the short, simple message, a call to accept Christ as Lord and Saviour was given. Nine people responded joyfully. There was a lot of clapping and celebration as they moved to the front of the room. I led the small group in a prayer of repentance, commitment and thanksgiving. A prayer of blessing followed.

The next stage of the service was filled with a number of truly amazing, culturally authentic forms of worship. Small groups of believers, usually two or four, sang songs based on Scripture as they performed a kind of Christian folk dance. It was incredible – a wonderful form of worship which instructed and edified the entire group. Everyone entered in and the joy was almost palpable.

When the service finally came to an end, the nine new believers gathered together for instruction. I was especially touched by one family. The husband had just committed his life to Christ. He along with his wife and their small one-year-old baby stood together. Their faces reflected the joy that Jesus pictured in his parable – the joy that would have overwhelmed the poor, the crippled, the blind and the lame as they heard the wonderful news that they had been invited to the banquet of their dreams.

Lord, help me respond to you and your grace with boundless gratitude and sheer joy. May my life reflect the kind of joy that would have welled up inside the poor, the crippled, the blind and the lame as they realized the invitation to the banquet truly was directed to them. And Lord, send me out to the country roads and rural lanes so that I might declare the gracious and joyful invitation, 'Come, everything is now ready.'

Meditation #46:
Pleasing God rather than People

You know, brothers, that our visit to you was not a failure.
We had previously suffered and been insulted in Philippi,
as you know, but with the help of our God we dared to tell
you his gospel in spite of strong opposition. For the appeal
we make does not spring from error or impure motives, nor
are we trying to trick you. On the contrary, we speak as men
approved by God to be entrusted with the gospel. We are
not trying to please men but God, who tests our hearts. You
know we never used flattery, nor did we put on a mask to
cover up greed – God is our witness. We were not looking
for praise from men, not from you or anyone else (1 Thes.
2:1–6).

On 25 November 2002, I met with Brother Cai, the leader
of the Yin Shang house church network. Persecution was
a major topic of our discussion. One of Brother Cai's colleagues had been arrested a few weeks earlier and he was
still in prison. After we prayed for this man, Brother Cai
noted that just two days previously the Chinese
government had conducted high-level meetings with
various departments within their bureaucracy in which
they discussed their policy towards the house churches.
The government officials concluded that they would
strictly enforce new measures which demanded that all
house churches register with the government. The
government attempted to present this new policy as an

opportunity for house church groups to register and receive government recognition.

During our time together, Brother Cai received many calls from his colleagues asking how they should respond to the new policies. Brother Cai said they would not register, but wait and watch how things developed. He felt that this new policy actually represented a new wave of persecution, not a new opening. In the past, the government had often issued fines for failure to register. Now, Brother Cai stated, they were intent on arresting people who did not comply. Brother Cai indicated that they would only register if there were no conditions placed upon them. He stated that currently the government was asking for the names of leaders, the number and names of believers, and the location of their meetings. This was not acceptable to him. Approximately one month after our meeting, Brother Cai was arrested and imprisoned. He is, as far as I know, still being held in prison.

Lord, I am humbled when I think of the commitment of people like Brother Cai. He could submit to the government regulations and walk away from prison a free man. And yet he will not, for he is a man of conviction. He is concerned not so much about what the government officials will say or do; rather, he is concerned about what is right in your eyes. Lord, help me to be a person of integrity. I confess that all to often I am overly concerned about how other people view me. Lord, help me be more concerned about how I am viewed in your eyes.

Meditation #47:
Preaching in Prison

The crowd joined in the attack against Paul and Silas, and the magistrates ordered them to be stripped and beaten. After they had been severely flogged, they were thrown into prison, and the jailer was commanded to guard them carefully. Upon receiving such orders, he put them in the inner cell and fastened their feet in the stocks.

About midnight Paul and Silas were praying and singing hymns to God, and the other prisoners were listening to them. Suddenly there was such a violent earthquake that the foundations of the prison were shaken. At once all the prison doors flew open, and everybody's chains came loose. The jailer woke up, and when he saw the prison doors open, he drew his sword and was about to kill himself because he thought the prisoners had escaped. But Paul shouted, 'Don't harm yourself! We are all here!'

The jailer called for lights, rushed in and fell trembling before Paul and Silas. He then brought them out and asked, 'Sirs, what must I do to be saved?'

They replied, 'Believe in the Lord Jesus, and you will be saved – you and your household' (Acts 16:22–31).

My first encounter with the Word of Life house church came in Beijing in October 1998. At that time, I had the joy of meeting with a group of their leaders. The eight leaders (who came from their ministry posts in various parts of China) were, with one exception, all young – in their mid- to late-twenties. Most, however, had already been preaching for close to ten years. Seven of the eight were women. All but one had been in prison. One young lady who had been arrested along with Peter Xu (the group's founder and leader) the previous year, had only recently been released from prison.

A colleague of mine asked one young lady, Sister Chen, if she had been mistreated in prison. In a very matter of fact way, she answered, 'Yes, they beat me.' Sister Chen recounted how the prison officials tried to prevent her from preaching or praying: they beat her and shocked her with an electric baton in the chest. In spite of these difficulties, she continued to minister to those around her in the prison. One prostitute was healed and accepted Jesus as her Lord and Saviour. A number of others also became Christians as a result of Sister Chen's witness. On one occasion a guard attempted to rape her, but as she cried out in prayer, the guard fell unconscious and had to be taken to the hospital.

Later, as I spoke with Sister Chen, I learnt that she had memorized large amounts of the New Testament, including the Gospel of John, the book of Acts, Romans and Revelation, because when she was in prison they took her Bible away. She wanted to be prepared for the next opportunity she had to preach in prison.

The testimonies I heard that day were incredibly inspiring. They were filled with many stories of miraculous intervention, but I was particularly moved by the story of Sister Chen's prison cell becoming a house church.

Lord, I praise you for the way that you enable your servants to glorify your name in any circumstance. I rejoice at your faithfulness and protection in the life of Sister Chen and her colleagues. I pray that you would continue to use them mightily in China to build your church. And Lord, help me face adversity with the same kind of courage and joy as that modelled by Sister Chen, Paul and Silas. Whether it be in a prison cell or a cancer ward, give me strength to sing, pray and preach of your goodness.

Meditation #48:
A Rare and Precious Treasure

I seek you with all my heart;
   do not let me stray from your commands.
I have hidden your word in my heart
   that I might not sin against you.
Praise be to you, O LORD;
   teach me your decrees.
With my lips I recount
   all the laws that come from your mouth.
I rejoice in following your statutes
   as one rejoices in great riches.
I meditate on your precepts
   and consider your ways.
I delight in your decrees;
   I will not neglect your word (Ps. 119:10–16).

The service had just finished. I was in a large, crowded
TSPM church in a major city in China. As I turned
towards the aisle, I noticed the middle-aged couple
behind me. In their Mao suits they seemed a little out of
place. Most city dwellers had discarded their Mao suits
years ago. Moreover, their clothes were worn and
tattered. It was evident that these people were not locals,
but visitors from the village. Intrigued, I introduced
myself and asked if they were from out of town. Their
faces beamed at my small gesture of friendship. They told
me that they had come from a village located in a remote

part of our province, and that their journey to the city had taken three days. I knew their journey must have been a hard one. It had probably involved walking long distances and sitting for hours on hot, crowded buses. Curious as to why they had made such a difficult journey, I pressed further. They then revealed the purpose of their trip: they had come to the city to buy Bibles for the believers in their village.

It is true that Bibles can be purchased in most major cities in China, and at very reasonable prices. In our city one US dollar will buy a very nice, hard cover Bible containing both the Old and New Testaments. But this is only part of the story. It is also true that in our city of over three million people there is only one, small bookshop – a little room located in the local TSPM office – where Bibles can be purchased. Sometimes Bibles can be purchased in TSPM churches after the completion of a service, but you will never find them in public bookshops. Bibles are only available in some government recognized churches or in small, out of the way shops, associated with the TSPM.

The real problem, then, is that Bibles are not readily accessible to most believers. Although in the cities Bibles are generally available for purchase, it is usually very difficult to find the designated locations where they are sold. Additionally, most of these Bibles never make it out to the villages. The dearth of Bibles in rural areas is especially acute.

I was not surprised to hear this couple's story. I was, however, deeply moved as I thought of the difficulty of their journey and the numerous Bibles sitting on book-shelves in my home.

Some time after this incident, a Chinese evangelist from the countryside, Brother Long, stopped by my office. His words of greeting included a brief reference to a gift. I was too preoccupied with offering hospitality to pay much attention to this remark. Brother Long was carrying a burlap bag, but I assumed that it contained his necessities. Brother Long often travels to outlying villages, encouraging the saints and delivering Bibles. When possible, I give him Bibles to take to the leaders of the village churches. On this occasion, we sat down in my office and talked about his upcoming trip. The burlap bag was positioned next to my chair. Providentially, I had a dozen Chinese Bibles that I was able to give to him that day. I will never forget the joy that lit up his face as he saw the Bibles. On more than one occasion he has shed tears when I have handed him a stack of Bibles. Suddenly, this joyous scene was interrupted by a surprising sight. I leapt to my feet as I saw the burlap bag begin to roll across my office floor. After I regained my composure, I heard the clucking sounds. The bag contained my gift: a live chicken.

Lord, I confess that I take for granted so many of the blessings which you have showered upon me. I acknowledge that I have abundant access to your word, yet I do not study and meditate upon it as I should. When I hear of people like the couple above who must travel great distances simply to obtain a Bible, I am humbled. I have many Bibles, but too often I fail to read them. Lord, help me cherish your word. Help me value it in the way my Chinese brothers and sisters do – as a rare and precious treasure.

Meditation #49:
A Chinese Parable

But he wanted to justify himself, so he asked Jesus, 'And who is my neighbour?'

In reply Jesus said: 'A man was going down from Jerusalem to Jericho, when he fell into the hands of robbers. They stripped him of his clothes, beat him and went away, leaving him half-dead. A priest happened to be going down the same road, and when he saw the man, he passed by on the other side. So too, a Levite, when he came to the place and saw him, passed by on the other side. But a Samaritan, as he travelled, came where the man was; and when he saw him, he took pity on him. He went to him and bandaged his wounds, pouring on oil and wine. Then he put the man on his own donkey, took him to an inn and took care of him. The next day he took out two silver coins and gave them to the innkeeper. "Look after him," he said, "and when I return, I will reimburse you for any extra expense you may have."

'Which of these three do you think was a neighbour to the man who fell into the hands of robbers?'

The expert in the law replied, 'The one who had mercy on him.'

Jesus told him, 'Go and do likewise' (Lk. 10:29–37).

Rush hour in our city is something to behold. Thousands upon thousands of cyclists pack into crowded bike lanes and pedal home. The number of buses and cars that clog the already congested streets has risen dramatically in the last few years, but bicycles still represent the standard mode of transportation.

One afternoon my wife and I were pedalling home on a busy street. We were part of a human current, swept along by the flow of countless bicycles. As we crossed a major intersection we saw a man in front of us, clearly unconscious, sprawled out on top of his toppled bicycle in the middle of the narrow, ten-foot wide, bike lane. With some difficulty, the sea of bicycles simply parted and passed around him as if nothing had happened. Not one person stopped to help. We were astounded at this callousness. We quickly dismounted and attempted to help the poor man, even as some shouted to us not to bother. After moving him to the pavement, I rushed over to a small clinic across the street. When I returned with a doctor and a stretcher, the man was already conscious and talking with my wife. After a brief conversation with the doctor and a word of thanks to us, he re-entered the stream of bicycles and disappeared into the distance.

It took me some time to put this incident in perspective. I had always viewed Chinese people as very gracious and hospitable. Our Chinese friends were always incredibly cordial hosts. Moreover, the Chinese we know value relationships with family members and friends in a way that often puts us in the West to shame, so I struggled to understand this experience.

In time, however, the matter became clear to me. There are spheres of relationship in China: family, friends, colleagues and guests. If you fit into one of these categories you will be treated with great kindness. However, if you do not, essentially you do not exist. The same people who are tremendously kind to their friends or guests, will without giving it a second thought pedal by an unknown cyclist in need. Everything depends on relationship (*guanxi*).

I have pondered what is at the root of this particular cultural trait. The sheer volume of people in China tends to encourage the Chinese to compartmentalize their lives. After all, if you feel responsible for everyone, your day would be one endless series of interruptions. With people pressing in on every side it is better to focus on those whom you know, the relationships that are clearly defined. But it is precisely here where I see a deeper, more fundamental influence upon Chinese perceptions. Here we see the difference between Confucius and Jesus.

Not long after the bicycle incident I found myself teaching an evening course on the parables of Jesus for a group of house church leaders. It was exciting to see this eager group's response to these provocative and powerful stories. When we came to the parable of the good Samaritan, I pointed out that here Jesus was addressing a question common in his day: to whom must I show compassion and concern? Does my responsibility extend to people in my family, my tribe, or my ethnic group? How large is the sphere of my responsibility? I then shared my experience in the bicycle lane with the group. Smiles came to their faces and their eyes gleamed with awareness. They knew exactly what I was talking about. We all agreed – in the Chinese context Jesus' teaching is especially striking, especially relevant. For with this short story Jesus declares that we cannot carefully compartmentalize our lives. He calls for us to see our sphere of responsibility in the largest possible terms. He challenges us to show compassion to those in need regardless of the nature of our relationship, regardless of the barriers that so often divide. The next time a cyclist falls in our city, I know a group of Chinese believers who will not simply pedal on by.

Lord, you are the Creator, and you have created every culture on this planet. Every culture has something within it that is good, something that reflects your character. And yet I acknowledge that because of sin, every culture, including my own, has elements that need to be transformed. But I rejoice because you are at work redeeming and transforming people from countless cultural groups of the world. Through the lives of these people, you are transforming their cultures. You are changing patterns of behaviour and ways of looking at others. Lord, I rejoice at what you are doing in China. I ask that the transformed lives of millions of Chinese Christians would be a strong testimony to all and that through their lives this nation would be greatly blessed. And Lord, I pray that you would change me. Help me lay aside attitudes that serve to separate me from others. Let me follow you and show compassion to all who stand in need, because they are loved by you. They are my neighbours.

Meditation #50:
Mixed Responses

Moved by the Spirit, he went into the temple courts. When the parents brought in the child Jesus to do for him what the custom of the Law required, Simeon took him in his arms and praised God, saying:

'Sovereign Lord, as you have promised,
    you now dismiss your servant in peace.
  For my eyes have seen your salvation,
    which you have prepared in the sight of all people,
  a light for revelation to the Gentiles
    and for glory to your people Israel.'

The child's father and mother marvelled at what was said about him. Then Simeon blessed them and said to Mary, his mother: 'This child is destined to cause the falling and rising of many in Israel, and to be a sign that will be spoken against, so that the thoughts of many hearts will be revealed. And a sword will pierce your own soul too' (Lk. 2:27–35).

Recently I had the joy of preaching in a local house church. Around 60 people packed into the small sitting room of the tiny apartment. The whole place was a sea of faces, as people sat pressed together on tiny wicker stools. Others peered in from doors that led to adjoining rooms. The service began with prayer and singing. The believers enthusiastically joined the worship leader as she sang a number of distinctively Chinese, but clearly Christian choruses. The atmosphere was informal and filled with joy. I then shared a simple message from the gospels. More singing and testimonies followed.

At this point the service was suddenly interrupted by loud screams and yelling. Several loud blows shook the front door. At first I thought a very serious domestic fight was taking place and that it had spilled out into the hallway. Then I was told that this was the response of a disgruntled neighbour who often reacted to their meetings in this way. I believe the adversary was very likely demon-possessed. The yelling, screaming and belligerence had a surreal quality to it. It was not natural. I was later told that this neighbour had complained to the local government leaders and asked that they put a stop to these Christian meetings. The leaders replied, 'There is religious freedom in China. These people are Christians and they have the right to meet together.' Of course, this is not the usual response of government leaders in China, but it was wonderful to hear of this supportive stance.

Initially, the church leaders felt that we should end our meeting and not risk possibly agitating the neighbours further. However, after further consideration, the decision was made to continue. I was encouraged by this, for I had a sense that God had more in store for us that night. The meeting continued and, in spite of the opposition, there was a special sense of God's presence. One young man in particular was especially responsive. He was moved by the worship and the message. I had the joy of leading him to the Lord that night.

The following night our family participated in another service. After several testimonies, people virtually ran forward in order to accept Jesus as Lord and Saviour. After the service, my daughters commented on how inspiring it was to see the hunger of the people. I couldn't help but think of the striking contrast: angry, screaming denunciations on the one hand; and people rushing forward to commit their lives to Christ on the other. The message of the gospel often evokes very different responses. It can generate irrational and often demonically inspired opposition, but it also ignites a deep hunger for and sensitivity to the presence of God. Simeon's prophecy announced over the child Jesus is still being fulfilled today with clear reference to the entire world (not simply Israel), 'This child is destined to cause the falling and rising of many in Israel, and to be a sign that will be spoken against, so that the thoughts of many hearts will be revealed' (Lk. 2:34–35).

Lord, I praise you for you are at work liberating your creation. No demonic power is too great for you. No opposing force can stand in your way. In the face of every obstacle, your kingdom advances. Although some stand opposed, your message continues to bring healing and life. Lord, I declare my allegiance to you this day. Help me be responsive to your leading, receptive to your word. Birth within me a fresh hunger for your presence. Strengthen me, so that even in the face of opposition, I will stand firm for you.

Meditation #51:
Preaching on an Empty Stomach

I am not saying this because I am in need, for I have learned
to be content whatever the circumstances. I know what it is
to be in need, and I know what it is to have plenty. I have
learned the secret of being content in any and every
situation, whether well fed or hungry, whether living in
plenty or in want. I can do everything through him who
gives me strength (Phil. 4:11–13).

One young Chinese evangelist shared how when she was
just 18 years old she began to go out and preach in
outlying villages. On one occasion she and two co-
workers travelled to a remote mountain area and stayed
with a family in a village there. They had travelled all day
with nothing to eat. The next morning the evangelist
expected to eat breakfast together with her companions,
but their hosts were not Christians and they did not offer
them any food. Without food, they went out and picked
potatoes with their host in the field. They used their bare
hands, for no tools were available.

At noon, again they were not offered food; rather, the
host simply returned to his house and ate there, not
inviting them to come. The young evangelist broke down
and cried out to God. She had expected to be treated in
the same manner her mother had received evangelists in
their home. As she spoke of the cruel way that their hosts
were treating them, her other two colleagues (both older

and more mature) emphasized that their hosts had accepted them into their home. They should be grateful. So they prayed together in the field. That afternoon they again worked in the fields.

Later, the band of evangelists were able to share the gospel with the host family. The family responded to their message with genuine repentance and became followers of Jesus. Today, a large house church meets in that place and the members of the host family are pillars in the church. They now remember with great fondness the first time they heard the gospel from three hungry evangelists, and my evangelist friend remembers the lessons God taught her that day as she picked potatoes with an empty stomach.

Lord, I give you thanks, for you have showered your blessings upon me. You welcome me into your presence as your child. You fill me with your joy and peace. You lead and guide me. You have called me to be part of your glorious mission in the world, and you give me the strength to serve you. Lord, let me live with a heart overflowing with thanksgiving. Enable me to be content wherever you place me. Whether, materially speaking, I have much or little, help me rejoice in the knowledge that I am following you.

Meditation #52:
The Cleansing Stream

"'For I will take you out of the nations; I will gather you from all the countries and bring you back into your own land. I will sprinkle clean water on you, and you will be clean; I will cleanse you from all your impurities and from all your idols. I will give you a new heart and put a new spirit in you; I will remove from you your heart of stone and give you a heart of flesh. And I will put my Spirit in you and move you to follow my decrees and be careful to keep my laws. You will live in the land I gave your forefathers; you will be my people, and I will be your God.'" (Ezek. 36:24–28).

Spirit of the Lord Anoint Us Again

The heavens open, the heavens open
  The Holy Spirit descends like a dove
Anointing you and renewing me
  Life's living water flows like a river, like a stream
Heavenly dove, Spirit of Truth, come dwell forever in our
    hearts
  Take hold of our hands and lead us into the water,
Time and time again
  Like a deer thirsts for water from the stream
Our spirits yearn constantly for the Spirit of the Lord
  Anoint our hearts and revive us again.[1]

---

[1] Lu Xiaomin, *Sounds of the Heart*, 197 (Song #173).

The Holy Spirit is Moving in this Place

> Hallelujah, the Holy Spirit is moving in this place
> > Like the first rain after the Spring thunder
> It saturates the ground, it saturates the ground
> > Our heart's door to the Lord we open wide
> Like sunflowers turning towards the radiance of the sun
> > The love of the Lord envelopes us
> Like dew covers the green grass
> > Like on a Summer day in the desert,
> When one finds shade and a cool stream
> > We worship and praise Him
> The Holy Spirit is moving in this place.[2]

Lord, I worship you, for you delight to cleanse, empower, and renew. Your Spirit comes upon me like a cleansing stream, washing away the impurities in my life. You have taken away my hardened heart and replaced it with one that is receptive to you. In the midst of my weakness, your Spirit comes and grants me strength so that I might follow you. Lord, I open my heart to your Spirit's renewing work. Cleanse me. Change me. Use me.

---

[2] Lu Xiaomin, *Sounds of the Heart*, 529 (Sing #472).

Scripture Index

The Old Testament

The New Testament

Luke Wesley

Luke Wesley (a pen name) is a missionary who has lived and served in China for most of the past decade. He speaks Mandarin fluently, has ministered extensively in house church groups and rural TSPM churches and is the Field Director for the China Training Network, a Christian missions organization dedicated to the training of pastors, evangelists and church-planters in China.

For more information, you may contact Luke Wesley at: chinatrainingnetwork@mchsi.com

Or you may write to:

Luke Wesley, The China Training Network, 3237A E. Sunshine #111 Springfield, MO 65804, USA

By the same author –

The Church in China: Persecuted, Pentecostal, and Powerful

'At last a knowledgeable Pentecostal confirms that a great part – perhaps even the majority – of China's Protestants are Pentecostal or Pentecostal-like, and this on the basis of thorough field research

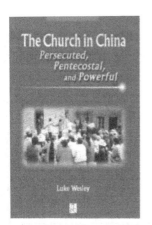

and by an author who speaks Chinese ... All in all a most useful book. The author has researched an extremely difficult field. Thank you, whoever you are (Luke Wesley is a pen-name).'

From the foreword by Walter J. Hollenweger, Former Professor of Mission, University of Birmingham

To order, contact the China Training Network at chinatrainingnetwork@mchsi.com or the Asian Journal of Pentecostal Studies at ajps@apts.edu.

In October of 1967 Pastor Richard Wurmbrand, along with his wife Sabina, founded a non-profit missionary organization to bring assistance to persecuted Christians around the world.

Today, **The Voice of the Martyrs, Inc.** continues to carry out this work. For more information about the mission activities, please write to **THE VOICE OF THE MARTYRS** at the addresses below.

USA:	P. O. Box 443 Bartlesville, OK 74005-0443
CANADA:	P. O. Box 117 Port Credit Mississauga, Ontario L5G 4L5 Canada
AUSTRALIA:	P. O. Box 250 Lawson, NSW 2783 Australia
NEW ZEALAND:	P. O. Box 5482 Papanui, Christchurch New Zealand
UNITED KINGDOM:	Release International P. O. Box 54 Orpinton BR5 9RT United Kingdom